SEVEN GOSPELS

SEVEN GOSPELS

THE MANY LIVES OF CHRIST IN THE BOOK OF MORMON

Adam S. Miller | Rosalynde F. Welch

Salt Lake City, Utah

Visit us at deseretbook.com

Library of Congress Cataloging-in-Publication Data

Names: Miller, Adam S., author. | Welch, Rosalynde, author.
Title: Seven gospels: the many lives of Christ in the Book of Mormon / Adam S. Miller, Rosalynde F. Welch.
Description: Salt Lake City, Utah: Deseret Book, [2023] | Includes bibliographical references and index. | Summary: "Latter-day Saint scholars Adam S. Miller and Rosalynde F. Welch identify and discuss seven gospels of Jesus Christ in the Book of Mormon"—Provided by publisher.
Identifiers: LCCN 2023025123 | ISBN 9781639932054 (trade paperback)
Subjects: LCSH: Jesus Christ—In the Book of Mormon. | Jesus Christ—Mormon interpretations. | Book of Mormon—Criticism, interpretation, etc.
Classification: LCC BX8627. M54 2023 | DDC 232—dc23/eng/20230609
LC record available at https: //lccn.loc.gov/2023025123

Printed in the United States of America
PubLitho, Draper, UT

10 9 8 7 6 5 4 3 2 1

For J. Spencer Fluhman
A Brother in Christ,
a Disciple-Scholar,
a Defender of the Faith

— CONTENTS —

"Brothers and sisters, in this Church, we believe in the divine potential of all of God's children and in our ability to become something more in Christ. In the Lord's timing, it is not where we start but where we are headed that matters most."

—Elder Clark G. Gilbert

— INTRODUCTION —

In his landmark October 1986 general conference talk, "The Book of Mormon—Keystone of Our Religion," President Ezra Taft Benson urged Latter-day Saints, as Christian disciples, to make the Book of Mormon central to their lives. He described the book as being "more important than any of the inventions that have come out of the industrial and technological revolutions" and as being "of greater value to mankind than even the many wonderful advances we have seen in modern medicine." The Book of Mormon, he taught, is more powerful than any machine. And as a witness of Christ, the Book of Mormon is potent medicine for the spiritual sicknesses that weaken us individually and cripple us collectively.

However, President Benson also added a warning. The early Saints were cautioned not to trifle with sacred things (see Doctrine and Covenants 6:12). They were told that if they treated the Book of Mormon lightly, the whole Church would come under condemnation (see Doctrine and Covenants 84:54–57). "Has the fact that we have had the Book of Mormon with us for over a century and a half made it seem less significant to us today?" President Benson asked. "If the early Saints were rebuked for treating the Book of Mormon lightly, are we under any less condemnation if we do the same?"[1]

In this same prophetic spirit, President Russell M. Nelson titled his October 2017 general conference talk "The Book of Mormon:

What Would Your Life Be Like without It?" This is a pivotal question. Can we imagine our lives without the Book of Mormon? How different would those lives be without the Restoration's founding witness of Christ? But President Nelson, too, asked us to consider what our lives would be like if we more deeply engaged *with* the Book of Mormon. What if, instead of reading the Book of Mormon casually or occasionally, we dedicated ourselves to searching for Christ in its pages? At the very least, President Nelson promised, "As you daily immerse yourself in the Book of Mormon, you can be immunized against the evils of the day."

For our part, as the authors of this book, we can't imagine our lives without the Book of Mormon. And faithful to this prophetic counsel, we've made lifelong efforts to take these promises seriously.

As disciples and as scholars, we've dedicated our hearts and minds to the work of reading the Book of Mormon, loving the Book of Mormon, and finding Christ in the Book of Mormon.

As disciples, our work has been daily and devotional. But we've also spent the past decade working closely with J. Spencer Fluhman at Brigham Young University's Neal A. Maxwell Institute for Religious Scholarship, engaged in this same uncompromisingly faithful work as scholars. Studying the Book of Mormon as scholars—especially with an eye single to Christ's ongoing reality rather than historical marginalia—we've worked to help fulfill Elder Maxwell's vision that "for a disciple of Jesus Christ, academic scholarship is a form of worship."[2] And in this respect, the work of disciple-scholarship enabled by the Maxwell Institute is, now more than ever, a rare gift in a world that struggles to believe.

Our hope is that this book will be a good example of the disciple-scholar's hybrid work—of careful study practiced as steadfast worship.

On one hand, this book is shaped by our scholarly training in literature, philosophy, and theology—disciplines that, despite their obvious limitations, help open unique perspectives on the Book of Mormon's witness of Christ. On the other hand, our aim is for this book to be useful to any disciple of Christ, scholar or not, who loves the Book of Mormon and hopes to deepen their faith.

Structurally, this book is organized based on two convictions. Our first conviction is that the Book of Mormon's powerful witness of Christ results, in part, from the wide chorus of diverse voices in the book who testify of Christ. Thus a study of seven witnesses of Christ composes the content of this book. And, second, the format of this book is based on our conviction that it's easier to appreciate the unique contributions of these many witnesses when we read the Book of Mormon together—collaboratively—as colleagues, disciples, and friends. To this end, the book is itself structured as a conversation in a series of open-ended letters passed back and forth between the coauthors, who are disciples, scholars, and friends.

Like the New Testament, the Book of Mormon bears witness of Christ's divinity and atonement through a variety of overlapping perspectives that use a range of similar, but not identical, images and vocabularies. And, like the New Testament, each of these different witnesses in the Book of Mormon might be described as a "gospel." The literal meaning of the New Testament word for "gospel" (*euangelion*) names each witness's proclamation as God's "good news" or the writer's "joyful announcement" of Christ's redemptive mission.

The core of the gospel is this joyful announcement: God the Father has sent into the world his Son, Jesus Christ, who is both human and divine. The Son has come to glorify the Father and to save the human family through his suffering, death, and resurrection. This core gospel is announced on nearly every page of the Book of Mormon. Jacob, the brother of Nephi, announced it as succinctly as any: "He cometh into the world that he may save all men if they will hearken unto his voice; for behold, he suffereth the pains of all men, yea, the pains of every living creature, both men, women, and children, who belong to the family of Adam" (2 Nephi 9:21).

In the New Testament and Book of Mormon, these core gospel announcements often appear as the center of a missionary lesson or a sermon, like Paul's letter to the Romans or the great address that Jacob delivers to the Nephites in 2 Nephi 9, quoted just above. But sometimes the core gospel announcement comes wrapped inside the story of the life of Jesus Christ. It makes sense to contextualize the good news of Jesus's identity and mission within the events of his mortal life. After all, it was through the events of his birth, ministry, and death that his mission was carried out. In the New Testament, we're given four of these gospels, four witnesses of the Savior's mission and redemption, wrapped in retellings of Christ's life: Matthew, Mark, Luke, and John. These written accounts are so central to the New Testament witness of Christ that they're often referred to simply as "the four Gospels."

When scholars and preachers speak of "the gospel" or "the gospel of Jesus Christ," they're referring to the core announcement. When they speak of "the Gospels" or "the Gospel according to Matthew" (or Mark, Luke, or John), they're typically referring to the written accounts found in the New Testament. President Gordon B. Hinckley, for instance, spoke of "the four gospels of the New Testament," adding that "there is a fifth which speaks with equal power. . . . It is found in this other testament which we call the Book of Mormon."[3]

Thus in this book, when we speak of "seven gospels" within the Book of Mormon, we are speaking of narratives of Christ's mortal life. The core gospel announcement is always the same, and it appears everywhere in the Book of Mormon. But we've focused especially on those places where this core announcement comes wrapped in the story of Christ's life, including accounts of his birth, his ministry, his death, and his resurrection. Though we've specifically identified seven of these witnesses in the Book of Mormon, there are certainly more. We've tried to choose witnesses who announce their good news from a variety of perspectives, witnesses whose lives represent a whole array of different circumstances and experiences: men and women, Nephites and Lamanites, kings and rebels, dreamers and readers, insiders and outsiders.

These seven accounts of Christ's life were crafted around a governing purpose: to kindle faith in Jesus Christ in the hearts of readers. Each author, led by inspiration, selected, arranged, and expressed the events of Christ's life so as to reach the hearts of his or her envisioned audience. Each carefully wrapped the core gospel announcement in a tailored retelling, and the results are seven passages of scripture that vary widely in shape, approach, and tone. Each gives us a unique portrait of Jesus, a singular perspective on the joyful news at the heart of the gospel of Christ.

When we pay closer attention to the details of each witness's proclamation of the good news, then the Book of Mormon's unified testimony of Christ begins to reveal unique insights. Reading deeply and carefully, we can learn to recognize the variations in perspective, experience, and vocabulary that characterize each witness's singular experience of Christ.

Considered collectively, the Book of Mormon bears powerful witness that, regardless of his disciples' personal differences, Christ is willing and able to show himself to all of us.

With respect to these seven Book of Mormon gospels, we expect that readers will find some of our choices obvious. But we also hope that in other cases readers will be surprised. The seven gospels studied here include

- the gospel of Mary, in 1 Nephi 11;
- the gospel of Benjamin, in Mosiah 3;
- the gospel of Abinadi, in Mosiah 15;
- the gospel of Alma, in Alma 7;

- the gospel of Abish, in Alma 19;
- the gospel of Samuel, in Helaman 14; and
- the gospel of the brother of Jared, in Ether 3.

While the gospel witnesses of towering prophetic figures like Nephi, Benjamin, Abinadi, Alma, Samuel, and the brother of Jared are likely to be familiar to readers, the inclusion of Mary (especially in relation to 1 Nephi 11) and Abish on this list of seven gospels may be surprising. But if your experience is anything like our own, we also expect that you'll find the chapters dedicated to the humble testimonies of these extraordinary women to be two of the most rewarding, inspiring, and Christ-centered in the book. Mary and Abish both prove the gospel rule that "by small and simple things are great things brought to pass; and small means in many instances doth confound the wise" (Alma 37:6).

In 1 Nephi 11, we investigate how Nephi's vision of the "condescension of God" opens a window onto Mary's own experience of God's good news. And when we foreground those elements of Nephi's vision that speak to Mary's own experience of God, we discover a gospel that speaks to her unique experience of God's love as a mother who was called to give birth to the Son of God and then had to allow that child to grow up, leave her home, suffer, and die.

In Mosiah 3, we look at the gospel of King Benjamin, a gospel told from the perspective of a battle-scarred king nearing his death. Benjamin's good news is delivered by an angel in the night, and that message centers on how the shedding of Christ's blood redeems our shared human experience of weakness and mortality.

In Mosiah 15, we turn to the gospel of Abinadi, who unlike Benjamin, is a rebel rather than a king. Bound in chains, Abinadi delivers the good news to King Noah's court at Abinadi's trial, and his witness grows organically from his interpretation of Isaiah's poetic and messianic prophecies, prophecies that draw a surprising connection between Christ's divine kingship and his capacity for meekness, silence, and suffering without yielding.

In Alma 7, we reflect on the gospel of Alma, delivered to the people of Gideon only after Alma, like Christ, willingly gives up his judgment seat to focus on preaching the good news of mercy and redemption. Memorably, Alma's account of the good news explains why, in an effort to save us not only from our sins but also from our sicknesses and infirmities, Christ had to suffer these things with us "according to the flesh" (Alma 7:12–13).

In Alma 19, we linger with Mormon's brief description of Abish, a Lamanite servant, who was converted unto the Lord—long before Ammon's arrival—by a remarkable vision of her father. We look at how pivotal Abish's anticipatory conversion is to the birth of Lamanite Christianity, and we treat her experience as a powerful case study of conversion and of the bare essentials needed to undergo the transformation promised by Christ.

In Helaman 14, we consider the gospel of Samuel. Like Abish, Samuel is a Lamanite and, especially as a Lamanite, his prophetic message is unwelcome among the Nephites. Samuel's reception isn't improved by the fact that his announcement of God's good news comes packaged with both dramatic prophecies of wholesale destruction and bold predictions of striking cosmic signs.

And finally, in Ether 3, we circle back to what is, chronologically, the Book of Mormon's earliest gospel: the gospel of the brother of Jared. Ironically, the years separating the brother of Jared's life from Christ's mortal birth don't distance him from direct contact with God. Alone among the gospels considered here, the gospel of the brother of Jared doesn't deliver a message *about* Christ's coming life or work. Rather, the brother of Jared parts the veil and *meets* Christ, only to discover that Christ's premortal spirit already bears the distinct image of his future mortal flesh.

Through our letters to one another, we move from one gospel to the next, building as we go. Without any predetermined end points, we let the Book of Mormon decide what comes next. We offer readings, trade insights, pull loose threads, ask questions, and share personal stories that bear witness to Christ's hand in our own lives. And we try, throughout, to model what it's like to *do* disciple-scholarship as a shared and vital work.

We hope that as you read these letters, you'll get a feel for the differences in our voices, scholarly backgrounds, and life experiences. But we especially hope you'll get a feel for the real-world substance of our long-time friendship and for how that friendship is itself crucial to the work of finding Christ in the Book of Mormon, not despite the differences between us but because of them.

There is, of course, nothing definitive about the work we do here. Our work is scholarly and exploratory, not authoritative. Take what is useful and leave the rest. If this book aids your own efforts to read the Book of Mormon more carefully and prayerfully—that is, more as an act of worship—then we'll have achieved our goal.

And if this book prompts you to do more of this same collaborative work—together, with friends and loved ones of your own, in writing or in person—then we'll be glad to count you, too, as friends.

Adam S. Miller
Rosalynde Frandsen Welch
October 2023

— CHAPTER 1 —

The Gospel of Mary

1 NEPHI 11

Nephi is caught away in the Spirit to a high mountain, where he is shown the things his father Lehi saw in a dream. Nephi asks for the interpretation of the shining tree, and an angel shows him Mary of Nazareth. She is presently carried away in the Spirit and reappears with a child in her arms. Nephi is taught by the angel about the condescension of God, the divine love that bears fruit in the person and ministry of Jesus Christ. Nephi sees the glorious events of Christ's baptism, his teaching and healing of the afflicted, and the visitation of angels that would accompany his ministry. The angel then shows Nephi the judgment and crucifixion of the Lamb of God.

"Behold, the virgin whom thou seest is the mother of the Son of God, after the manner of the flesh. And it came to pass that I beheld that she was carried away in the Spirit. . . . And I looked and beheld the virgin again, bearing a child in her arms." (1 Nephi 11:18–20)

Adam,

When we came up with the idea for this book, we banked on a certain idea. We hoped that each of the seven accounts we dwell on would shine a different color of light on the life of Jesus Christ, a light filtered through the perspective, circumstance, and intention of each teller of the story. I think this is a sound expectation, based on the evidence of the four Gospels in the New Testament, each of which draws a distinct portrait of Christ. We'll see if it plays out that way. And in titling this chapter on 1 Nephi 11 "The Gospel of Mary," we've tipped our hand to another expectation: that the mother of Christ will be represented among these seven Book of Mormon perspectives. But some readers might be puzzled: 1 Nephi 11, an important chapter near the beginning of the book, contains Nephi's re-vision and interpretation of his father's prophetic dream. Why call it the gospel of Mary?[4]

The scriptures call for a practice of informed imagination to tease out the voices of women. I say "informed" because simply pasting our own thoughts onto the mouths of the women in these pages will just redouble their silence. Our only hope is to be exquisitely sensitive to clues in the text. But there's no doubt that we will also have to engage our imaginations, as much as our hearts and minds, to do justice to Mary and to what she knew about her son.

What captured my imagination and turned my mind to Mary in this passage is a simple phrase: "carried away in the Spirit" (1 Nephi 11:19). Nephi is shown an image of a woman, who the angel tells him is the mother of the Son of God, and then, Nephi reports, the woman is carried away in the Spirit for a time. Readers of the book have interpreted this reference to Mary in a variety of ways. In the Book of Mormon, the words "carried away in the Spirit" are most often used, especially in its early chapters, to describe what it's like to be given a vision. What if Mary were "carried away in the Spirit" in the same way Nephi was? What if Mary, too, were given a vision of the meaning of her son's life? And what if Nephi, for a time, prophetically saw what Mary saw in vision? Could there be traces of Mary's gospel in Nephi's record?

It's not a far-fetched idea. In fact, we know from Luke's Gospel that Mary was visited by an angel and told something of the son she would conceive (Luke 1:26–38). In this, Mary's experience was like that of Nephi, who was also visited by an angel who opened the future life of Christ to his view (1 Nephi 11:14). From Gabriel, Mary learned that her child would be called the Son of God, that he would hold David's throne and reign over his people Israel (Luke 1:32–33). If we conjecture that Nephi's account incorporates some of the content and meaning of Mary's vision—if we conjecture that Nephi saw some of what Mary saw, and that we, in turn, can see some of her vision as well—what else do we see through her eyes? What is Mary's gospel?

A mother's relationship to her child is a delicate thing, an ever-changing dynamic of coming and going, approach and rebuff, departure and return. My own kids span the spectrum from adolescence to young adulthood, and those comings and goings are the rhythm of my life. I picked up my son from the airport last night. He flew home from his cousin's house as an unaccompanied minor, so I met him at the arrival gate. It was a strange feeling, walking the concourse unencumbered by children and suitcases. It's been ten years since I last carried a child on my hip through an airport, but my bones still remember the shifting weight and heat, the off-center gravity. There were babies everywhere last night. Smiling babies, fussy babies, sleeping babies. A chubby one with brown eyes and curly hair stared at me from his mother's arms as we waited in the TSA line. The thing about babies is that they're easy to look at. They hold your gaze with such open freedom that it opens and frees you too.

I think stories also have a kind of rhythm, and I see in Mary's gospel the coming and going, the near-and-far rhythm of mother and child. After Mary has been carried away in the spirit, Nephi sees her again, this time carrying a child in her arms (1 Nephi 11:20). The angel says to Nephi, "Behold the Lamb of God" (1 Nephi 11:21). Nephi knows what he knows because of what the angel showed and told him. But there are some things you know best in your body. If my own experience as a mother offers any insight into Mary's, then I think Mary knows what she feels in her bones, the shifting weight of the child, the off-center gravity. There's no mention of a manger here: this is a child borne in arms. I imagine that Mary would have held her son close on her birth pallet and at the visit of the Magi; she would have carried him to the temple in Jerusalem and to safety in Egypt, away from Herod's mad decree. She would have held him as she fed him, bathed him, and calmed him.

The image of the Christ child in his mother's arms, unique to Mary's gospel, emphasizes the intimacy between the mother and her holy child, and thus it also heightens the poignancy of the sacrifice they both made in submitting to his atoning mission. This is the rhythm of motherhood: after coming is going; after nearness is distance. As the heft on her hip grew each day and time took its due, I think Mary would have known in her body what all parents know, you and I included: this is a child who will leave my arms and go into the world. Soon the weight will be replaced by an emptiness, like the ghost baby that rode my hip through the airport yesterday. This child is not mine, but the world's. Mary's parental intuition, however, would have taught her something vaster than yours or mine. Having been told by Gabriel of her child's divine identity (Luke 1:35), Mary would have had a motherly premonition of her child's coming departure into the world that would have revealed something about divinity itself. This is not a Lord who remains distant and removed from the world, like a holy hermit sequestered in a sacred fortress. This is a Lord who goes out among his people.

I'm making inferences about Mary's experience, of course, likening the scriptures to my own life in the process of "informed imagination" I mentioned above. For me, this kind of likening is valuable for the way it can partially reconstruct women's voices in the scriptures, but you and our readers should take it with a grain of salt. Still, what Mary may have intuited from holding the divine child in her arms, Nephi is shown directly by the angel. Twice the angel shows him the Son of God "going forth among the children of men" (1 Nephi 11:24, 31). Jesus leaves Mary's arms to be among his people. He goes out among the crowds who visit John to be baptized at the River Jordan; there he is baptized with them and, like them, buried in the water in a rehearsal of their future burials in the earth (1 Nephi 11:27). He goes out among the afflicted, healing and ministering (1 Nephi 11:28, 31). He goes out to disciples who fall at his feet and supplicate him, and he goes out to multitudes who cast him from among them (1 Nephi 11:24, 28). He goes out among them all.

Nephi and the angel see these scenes as manifestations of the condescension of God (1 Nephi 11:26). God's condescension is the love of Father and Son for their children: a love so great that a Father would send his own Son down to a world lying in wait; so great that a Son would descend from his place at the Father's side to die among his people, first in baptism and then on the cross. Considered in this way, the condescension of God is expressed in all scriptural images of Christ's descent to be with his people: divine fire entering the tabernacle (Exodus 40:34), the body of Jesus lying in the tomb as his soul liberated the captives in hell (Doctrine and Covenants 138:18, 23), the Man in white descending to the Nephite multitude (3 Nephi 11:8). And, too, it's a child carried in his mother's arms. It's fitting that in Mary's gospel the idea of divine condescension is introduced in conjunction with the image of the Nativity, which crystallizes the condescension of God perhaps better than any other image:

He came down to earth from heaven,
Who is God and Lord of all,
And his shelter was a stable,
And his cradle was a stall;
With the poor, and mean, and lowly,
Lived on earth our Savior holy.[5]

This is condescension.

Mary's motherly perspective, if we can find it in this text, adds an important nuance to our understanding of God's condescending love. We often picture Christ coming down to earth from heaven and then returning again to the heavenly throne where he will gather the faithful, as Nephi saw later in his vision (1 Nephi 13:37). We think of condescension as primarily an up-down or vertical movement. But I wonder if condescension looked and felt slightly different to Mary. She would have sensed that her son's direction was also a horizontal *out* and *into:* out of her arms and into the world, going forth among his people. The vertical axis of condescension emphasizes the power and glory of the pre- and postmortal Christ, at the top of his trajectory, and the humility of his descent into mortality. But to my mind, the horizontal axis of his movement from Mary's arms into the world emphasizes his essential solidarity with humankind, his willingness to be like us, among us, and for us.

These twin dimensions of condescension, Christ's "coming down" and "going forth," will prove to be important elements of the Book of Mormon's witness of Christ. Many of the other gospel accounts we'll be looking at later also use variations of these key phrases. Benjamin, Abinadi, Alma, and Samuel speak of Christ coming down (Mosiah 3:5; 15:1; Alma 7:7; Helaman 13:6). Benjamin, Abinadi, and Alma speak of Christ going forth (Mosiah 3:5; 13:34; Alma 7:11). Lamoni, with characteristic brevity, combines the two and proclaims that Christ will "come forth" (Alma 19:13). I love that the Book of Mormon's profound doctrine of the condescension of God originates at the beginning of Nephi's vision with the poignant image of Christ as a babe borne in Mary's arms.

The condescension of God, especially its horizontal direction, is expressed in 1 Nephi 11 not only in Christ's birth but also, supremely, in his death. Did you notice that Nephi doesn't see the Resurrection in his vision of the good news of Christ's life? The angel shows him the Crucifixion, and then the scene shifts to the persecution of early Christians. Of course, the Resurrection is implicit in the scene of Christ's postmortal visit to Nephi's people, and, after all, the angel had to hurry on (or Nephi did) to get to the extensive history of the covenant still to follow. But still, the end of this gospel is the judgment, crucifixion, and death of Christ. Christ's vertical return, his resurrection and ascension, are not directly described. This gospel ends on Friday. As I read it, that unexpected endpoint underscores both the importance of Christ's mortality and the gravity of his death. Christ took no shortcuts through mortal life in fulfilling his mission among humankind.

As I've been aiming to show in my imaginative exploration of Mary's experience, both Christ's birth and his death express divine condescension in that they follow the twin patterns of coming down and going forth. More, we can begin to grasp the significance of Christ's death from the very beginning, in the wonder of his mortal birth. This is why Mary matters so much to me here. Early in their conversation, the angel twice asks Nephi about what he knows. First he asks if Nephi knows the condescension of God. Nephi answers truthfully: "I know that he loveth his children; nevertheless, I do not know the meaning of all things" (1 Nephi 11:17). Nephi understands that God loves but doesn't yet understand how that love is expressed in Christ's coming down and going forth. He doesn't yet understand condescension.

As we've seen, the angel then shows him Mary, as she is carried away in the Spirit and reappears bearing a child in her arms, whom the angel identifies as the Lamb of God (1 Nephi 11:21). Teaching through juxtaposed patterns and images, the angel asks Nephi again about what he knows: "Knowest thou the meaning of the tree which thy father saw?" (1 Nephi 11:21). By calling to mind the beauty of the tree in Lehi's dream and associating it with the beauty of the mother he sees, Nephi recognizes that the fruit of the tree is symbolically equivalent to the child borne in her arms. And he begins to understand that both fruit and child embody divine condescension by giving themselves away to us completely, out of love and for our sakes. The vision of Mary, bearing her divine child in her arms, has taught him that condescension is Christ's coming down from heaven and going forth to the cross, and he answers the angel: "It is the love of God, which sheddeth itself abroad in the hearts of the children of men" (1 Nephi 11:22). He has understood the *how* of God's love: God's love is expressed through acts of self-shedding at Christ's birth and death (and continuously before, after, and between), and transmitted through the hearts of all people.

Adam, you and I both love the written word. Isn't there something perfect and crystalline about this phrase, "sheddeth itself abroad in the hearts of men"? Shortened in this way, and if you squint, it takes the form of iambic pentameter, the favored style of Shakespeare and Milton. But it's the word "shed" that really captures me. Although a similar verse appears in the New Testament, the idea of *love* being shed hasn't quite made it into an English idiom (see Romans 5:5). What kinds of things are shed? Skins are shed. Tears are shed. Light is shed. And blood is shed. This sounds like the scene of a birth, the messy and dangerous path by which Christ and his mother Mary agreed to bring the son of God bodily into the world so that he could live fully among us, one of us in every way except sin. And it sounds like the scene of a death: "This is my blood of the new testament, which is shed for many for the remission of sins" (Matthew 26:28). The love of God "sheds itself" through the willing birth and willing death of the child borne in Mary's arms.

I think this is the message of Mary's gospel. The condescension of God includes not only Christ's coming down from heaven, but his going forth among his people. Jesus came to earth to share all of human experience, minus sin, with and among his people, not merely to instruct us from a safe place at a comfortable distance. This truth gains special poignancy when seen from Mary's point of view. Mary appears as a faraway, revered figure in the other gospel accounts that we read together in the coming pages, but only here in 1 Nephi 11 do we get a glimpse of her own motherly perspective—incorporated, as we've surmised, as an element of Nephi's vision. Mary understands, as only a mother can, the personal cost at which the Savior, her babe in arms, will go into the world to spread the love of God through his ministry and his atonement. This, I think, is more than teary-eyed sentimentalism, though it certainly does move me as a mother myself. It's a significant contribution to our understanding of the mission of Jesus Christ and the condescension of God.

Rosalynde

"Knowest thou the meaning of the tree which thy father saw? And I answered him, saying: Yea, it is the love of God, which sheddeth itself abroad in the hearts of the children of men; wherefore, it is the most desirable above all things." (1 Nephi 11:21–22)

Rosalynde,

Like an expert audio engineer working at her soundboard, you've succeeded in dialing up the strength of Mary's voice, shifting it from the background to the foreground of Nephi's vision.

Your practice of informed imagination zeroed in on a crucial element of 1 Nephi 11—an element I'd never noticed—that makes it easier for us to overhear an approximation of Mary's own gospel: the fact that she, like Nephi, is "carried away in the Spirit" (1 Nephi 11:19).

When Nephi uses this same language to describe his experience in the chapter's opening verse—"as I sat pondering in mine heart I was caught away in the Spirit of the Lord"—he's clearly describing what it's like to have a vision of God (1 Nephi 11:1). But then Nephi, caught away in the Spirit, has a vision in which he, in turn, sees Mary herself carried away in the Spirit!

Nephi, it seems, has a vision of Mary being carried away in a vision. Embedded in Nephi's kaleidoscopic revelation is a tumbled fragment of Mary's own revelatory experience.

I love this idea. I love the idea that Nephi's vision of Mary's love opens onto Mary's vision of God's love. I love the idea of visions nested inside of visions, of voices nested inside of voices, all of them seeing and speaking through a shared experience of God's eyes and God's voice.

And I'm struck, too, by your account of what Mary is then uniquely positioned to see: God's condescension as something that unfolds not only as a (vertical) going down but as a (horizontal) "going forth"—out from Mary's arms and into the world until her Son is "lifted up upon the cross" and is "slain for the sins of the world" (1 Nephi 11:24, 33).

From the Father's perspective, the Son comes down and then the Father must let him be lifted up.

From the mother's perspective, the Son is placed in her arms and then Mary must let him go out and away.

This, too, is an essential dimension of the love of God, that love "which sheddeth itself abroad in the hearts of the children of men" (1 Nephi 11:22). This love includes a mother's love—Mary's love—for the Son. This love includes the ache of Mary's willing participation in her Son's sacrifice, consecration, and condescension. And, as you make clear, this ache—this phantom weight of a child no longer on your hip or in your arms—is the kind of consecrated sacrifice with which many mothers can identify.

To this sharp reading, let me try to add a pair of additional wrinkles.

First, I've been wondering if Nephi's account of his vision—enveloping as it does Mary's experience—might also evidence some traces of Luke 1–2, those chapters that, more than any other, record Mary's immediate experience of God's love while most directly preserving something of her voice.

In my estimation, there are a number of quilting points between 1 Nephi 11 and Luke 1–2 that, as we try to bring the gospel of Mary into sharper focus, might be worth our attention.

When the shepherds visit Mary, Joseph, and the baby Jesus and relay their angelic message, we're told that "Mary kept all these things, and pondered them in her heart" (Luke 2:19). When Nephi describes his own state of mind as 1 Nephi 11 opens, he says nearly the same: "As I sat pondering in mine heart I was caught away in the Spirit of the Lord" (1 Nephi 11:1). Here, both Mary and Nephi join a very short list of people in our scriptures who, we're explicitly told, "pondered in their hearts."

When Gabriel appears to Mary to announce her role as the mother of "the Son of the Highest," he proclaims: "Blessed art thou among women"—a blessing that Mary herself redoubles when she says that "all generations shall call me blessed" (Luke 1:32, 28, 48). When the Spirit first appears to Nephi in chapter 11, the Spirit praises God and says, "Blessed art thou, Nephi, because thou believest in the Son of the most high God" (1 Nephi 11:6).

In the "Song of Mary," commonly known as the Magnificat and preserved in Luke 1:46–55, Mary speaks for herself and tells us that "my soul doth magnify the Lord, and my spirit hath rejoiced in God my Saviour" (Luke 1:46–47). When Nephi describes the love of God as "most desirable above all things," his angelic guide can't help but interject: "Yea, and the most joyous to the soul" (1 Nephi 11:22–23).

Where Mary sings about how God has "scattered the proud in the imagination of their hearts" and "put down the mighty from their seats," Nephi sees that "great and spacious building" which was "the pride of the world" and how "it fell, and the fall thereof was exceedingly great" (Luke 1:51–52; 1 Nephi 11:35–36).

And where Mary affirms that God "helped his servant Israel" when he "exalted them of low degree" and "filled the hungry with good things," Nephi witnesses how "multitudes of people who were sick, and who were afflicted with all manner of diseases" were "healed by the power of the Lamb of God" (Luke 1:54, 52–53; 1 Nephi 11:31).

Primed by your reading, these possible points of correspondence stood out to me when I placed one text next to the other, whereas before they'd been all but invisible. By themselves they're nothing decisive—especially given the way these nested prophetic visions twist time's normally straight line into knots—but as part of an effort to hear Mary's voice, I find them hard to unsee.

To this delicate weave of correspondences, I want to also add a second, more substantial point.

To repeat your question: If we allow that something like the gospel of Mary is embedded in Nephi's own vision, then what is this gospel? What specific shape does the good news take? What unique aspects of Christ's life and atoning work are manifest in Mary's life, from Mary's point of view?

I think you're right to see Nephi's talk of "condescension" as the key to this chapter's distinctive presentation of the gospel of Jesus Christ.

In our scriptures, Nephi is the only person to use this term in connection with Jesus Christ, and outside of its two crucial uses in this chapter, he only uses it one other time—though, in this chapter, it would be more accurate to say that Nephi is the only person with whom an *angel* uses the term "condescension" to narrate the meaning of Christ's atoning work.

In 1 Nephi 11, this word is the angel's word. "Condescension" is the angel's own master term.

In the context of Nephi's vision, the word's sense stems directly from its pair of root meanings: *con*, meaning "with," and *descend*, meaning "to come down." To talk about the condescension of God is to talk about God's *coming down to be with us*. As another angel tells Mary's Joseph: "And they shall call his name Emmanuel, which being interpreted is, God with us" (Matthew 1:23). This is how he saves us, by being with us.

In chapter 11, the angel's two uses of the word "condescension" punctuate and structure Nephi's vision. These two uses are the deeply anchored nails on which the rest of the chapter hangs. The first time the angel uses the word, it's as a question: "Knowest thou the condescension of God?" (1 Nephi 11:16). And the second time the angel uses the word, it's as an imperative: "Look and behold the condescension of God!" (1 Nephi 11:26).

These two uses line up with the two images that, in preparation for the vision, Nephi was told he would see: "After thou hast beheld the tree which bore the fruit which thy father tasted, thou shalt also behold a man descending out of heaven, and him shall ye witness" (1 Nephi 11:7).

So we get two uses of the word *condescension* tied to two distinct but paired images: the image of the tree of life and the image of a man descending out of heaven. To decode the vision, Nephi must know their interpretation. He must discover how they fit together.

How is that interpretive gap bridged? What does the tree mean?

When Nephi is first shown the tree he sees that "the beauty thereof was far beyond, yea, exceeding of all beauty; and the whiteness thereof did exceed the whiteness of the driven snow," and he describes the tree as that "which is precious above all" (1 Nephi 11:8–9).

And when Nephi asks for "the interpretation thereof," he offers a clearly parallel (though not quite identical) description of "a virgin, and she was exceedingly fair and white" and "most beautiful and fair above all other virgins" (1 Nephi 11:11, 13, 15).

First, Nephi tells us that the tree of life is exceedingly beautiful, white, and precious above all.

And then Nephi tells us that Mary is exceedingly beautiful, white, and fair above all.

In sum, Nephi is shown the tree of life and then, when he asks for the interpretation of the tree, he's shown Mary.

What is the meaning of the tree of life? Or, better, *who* is the meaning of the tree of life?

While the tree of life is a powerful symbol with a complex history and many possible meanings, it seems to me that, in this instance at least, Mary is herself among the possible meanings of the tree. Here, Mary is linked with the tree of life. And as "the mother of the Son of God," she will bear in her womb—and in her arms (and on her hip)—the fruit of that tree, the man who will, after the manner of her flesh, descend from heaven to be with us and heal us and save us.

Mary bridges the gap between Nephi's initial vision of the tree of life and Nephi's subsequent vision of the man who descends from heaven to be with us. Mary is positioned as the missing link between them. And to see the meaning of this vision—to know the condescension of God—Nephi must learn how to see Mary.

Having seen Mary, Nephi is now ready to confidently answer the angel's next question. "Knowest thou the meaning of the tree which thy father saw?" the angel asks (1 Nephi 11:21). "Yea," Nephi exclaims, "it is the love of God, which sheddeth itself abroad in the hearts of the children of men; wherefore, it is the most desirable above all things" (1 Nephi 11:22). "Yea," the angel adds, "and the most joyous to the soul" (1 Nephi 11:23).

The tree, already associated with Mary, is now explicitly identified with "the love of God."

We might, then, offer the following reading. Mary is the tree of life. The tree of life is the love of God. The fruit of that tree is the Son of God. And this chain of carefully forged links describes the condescension of God.

What happens, though, if we try to see Nephi's vision—originally his father's vision—from Mary's perspective rather than Nephi's or Lehi's? What happens if we try to see this vision from the perspective of the tree itself?

If Mary is one meaning of the tree, then what would it feel like to be the tree? What would it feel like to *be* the love of God?

The "love of God" is, of course, a beautifully ambiguous phrase that can be read in either of two directions. Taken one way, it points toward God. Taken the other way, it points toward the person God loves.

The "love of Adam," for example, could refer to either the love that Adam (subjectively) feels for someone, or to the someone that Adam (objectively) loves—as in "the love of Adam is Gwen." The first reading may be more natural, but the second is always possible.

It's no surprise, then, that we tend to default to reading Nephi's "the love of God" as meaning the love that God (as a subject) feels for the children of men, a love that "sheds" itself abroad in their hearts, and a love that is embodied by the Son's ministry and mission. And this, clearly, is true.

But given how hard the angel has worked to link the tree to Mary, the second reading should also have some weight. In this case, it makes sense not only to ask: what would it feel like to be the tree and to feel the love that God feels for us? But further to ask: what would it feel like to be the object of God's love, to be the someone that God loves, and to be the one who, as a result of that love, becomes "the mother of the Son of God?"

We don't need to choose between these two readings. Both possibilities, perhaps inevitably, bleed into the other. And, what's more, I don't want to choose between them because I suspect that this slippage—this slippage between being the person God loves and being a vessel for God's love of another—is itself pivotal to experiencing God's love, to finding that "which is precious above all" and to experiencing that which is "most joyous to the soul" (1 Nephi 11:9, 23).

To partake of the fruit and experience God's love is always—in my experience—to find oneself both loved and filled with that same love for others. And if this is right, then Mary is herself a paradigm case of salvation: she both partakes of the fruit of the tree of life and *is* the tree of life.

Still, as it was for Nephi, part of Mary's experience is occluded for me. I see Mary "carried away in the Spirit," and then, "for the space of a time," I don't see her anymore (1 Nephi 11:19). I don't see her again until she appears on the far side of her own vision with, already, "a child in her arms" (1 Nephi 11:20). As a father, I'll never know what it's like to have a child growing inside of me, gathering life and strength in the womb.

But I can know, at least in part, the love that's required to let a child go out and away. I know something about what it's like to let a child go out and away after having, for so many years, held them on my lap and wrapped them in my arms. The strongest tactile memory I have as a father is of tucking my own sons, ages four and two, under my arms like footballs and carrying them up to bed. At least in this way, I have some idea of what it's like to be Mary—to be the tree of life, to be both the recipient and the giver of God's love.

Adam

— CHAPTER 2 —

The Gospel of Benjamin

MOSIAH 3

From his tower at the temple in Zarahemla, an aged King Benjamin exhorts his people to recognize their dependence on God and to keep the commandments. He announces a new king; his faltering body requires him to appoint his son Mosiah to the throne. Benjamin reports that an angel brought him glad tidings on the previous night: the time is not far distant when the Lord will come down from heaven and dwell among the children of men in a mortal body like theirs. The angel speaks to Benjamin of Christ's healing ministry and of his bodily temptation, pain, hunger, thirst, and fatigue. Because of his suffering, the people will fail to recognize his divinity, and he will be scourged, crucified, and slain. He will rise from the dead on the third day. Through the atoning blood of Christ, the natural man can become a saint—submissive, meek, humble, patient, and full of love.

"For behold, the time cometh, and is not far distant, that with power, the Lord Omnipotent who reigneth, who was, and is from all eternity to all eternity, shall come down from heaven among the children of men, and shall dwell in a tabernacle of clay." (Mosiah 3:5)

Adam,

The football hold is a classic of the dad bedtime genre. When our kids were small, my husband perfected an over-the-shoulder toss known as the "elephant dump," a technique inherited from his father. My own father would carry me upside down by the ankles, as I shrieked in delight down the long hallway of our California rambler. I can't imagine that he learned the technique from his dad, my grandpa, who certainly would have been away milking cows and doing chores at the bedtime hour. Later, Grandpa's evenings would have been spent attending city council meetings, or counseling ward members in the bishop's office. My grandpa was a bona fide, old-school pillar of his tiny farming community, a stalwart in city government, Church leadership and economic development. I grew up hearing about his storied introduction of modern irrigation techniques in their remote valley. He still lives, at 103 years old, in that same little valley. Grandma is still by his side. His hearing is about gone, and his vision is weak. He doesn't speak much anymore. But his hands, a landscape of valleys and scars and tendons like rock ridges, tell the story of his life's work.

The picture that Mary's gospel evokes for me is an image of her cradled arms and the sleeping child who rests there. King Benjamin's gospel shows me another kind of cradle, and the aged king who will soon rest in the arms of his mother earth. Benjamin's gospel, his capsule account of Christ's life from cradle to tomb and beyond, is delivered to him by an angel and then reported to his people from high atop a tower as part of his famous address. It's one of the most iconic scenes in the Book of Mormon: the old king—weak of voice, trembling in frame, infirm of body and mind—sustained by the breath of God to preach the good news of Christ, the new and everlasting king. "The time cometh, and is not far distant," Benjamin tells them, that their true king will come down and reign among them (Mosiah 3:5).

Benjamin's good news, like all accounts of Christ's mortal life in the Book of Mormon, is the promise of something that *will* happen, not the story of something that *has* happened, as in the New Testament Gospels. This changes the way Nephite Christians relate to the life of their promised King, in contrast to the early Christians of the Mediterranean world who look backward to understand the meaning of their Savior's life. But one thing remains the same: whether a gospel looks forward or backward to Christ, the truth of his life is given in the language of those who will speak and hear it. This language isn't merely the particular dialect of a people, but it also encompasses the images, ideas, and relationships that they understand.

Benjamin's gospel is, I think, a beautiful example of this kind of encompassing gospel translation. King Benjamin stands before his people as a powerful king who has nevertheless been ambushed by his own mortality: the affliction of his body, his vulnerability and suffering, are on full display. "For even at this time," he tells his people as he stands before them, "my whole frame doth tremble exceedingly while attempting to speak unto you" (Mosiah 2:30). His hands and face, probably a landscape as deeply carved as my grandfather's, tell the story of his life's work and his imminent death: King Benjamin "waxed old," we're told, and "must very soon go the way of all the earth" (Mosiah 1:9). Is it any wonder that Benjamin tells his people of Christ's healing of the deaf and blind? That he shows them Christ's pain and fatigue? Benjamin knows viscerally of age's encroachment; perhaps he knows its deafness and blindness. He knows viscerally a shadow of the affliction Christ will suffer. He teaches his people, not only with his words but with his trembling frame, of the King who will inhabit a tabernacle of clay.

"The time cometh, and is not far distant," Benjamin tells them (Mosiah 3:5). How soon did Benjamin think Christ would come? The angel didn't say. The birth of Christ would occur more than a hundred years in the future—not long on a cosmic scale, perhaps, but certainly far distant in relation to Benjamin's own time horizon. There is another appointed time coming for Benjamin, and this one surely is not distant (see Mosiah 1:9). The old king's imminent death frames his tidings of the new King's imminent birth.

But it's worth backing up for a moment to think about angels. An angel delivered the gospel of Mary to Nephi, just as an angel appeared to Benjamin bringing "glad tidings of great joy" (Mosiah 3:3). The nighttime setting of Benjamin's angelic visitation, as well as the text's echo of the "good tidings of great joy" delivered by an angel to shepherds abiding in the fields outside Bethlehem, invite us to put the gospel of Benjamin in conversation with the gospel of Luke (Luke 2:10). The two accounts share some of the basic features we'd expect in any recitation of the gospel, a word that, at root, simply means good or glad tidings. Both angels—the angel of Bethlehem and the angel of Zarahemla—deliver their tidings to the humble, announce the coming of Christ the Lord, and direct their message of joy to all people. And crucially, the Bethlehem angel tells the shepherds where and how to find this Savior: "For unto you is born this day in the city of David a Saviour, which is Christ the Lord. And this shall be a sign unto you; Ye shall find the babe wrapped in swaddling clothes, lying in a manger" (Luke

2:11–12). Could it be that the most important message of the angel to Benjamin and his people is, likewise, where and how to find the Savior?

The angel's instructions to the Bethlehem shepherds must have been surprising, even a little absurd. He tells them that the Messiah, anointed to the throne of David in the city of kings, will be found wrapped in swaddling clothes and lying in a manger, the most unkingly of cradles. This is the sign they give: you will know you have found the true king when you discover him in the most unexpected place. If the shepherds had gone seeking the Messiah on their own, probably the last thing they would have looked for is a newborn baby, still bound in the wrappings of his birth and placed in an animal's feedbox to rest. In fact, had they stumbled upon that strange scene, they might well have concluded that this unfortunate child, of all beings, could not be the Savior, true heir of David the king. And yet, in the angel's mouth, those humble features become the very sign that they have found him. The manger and the swaddling clothes are both the disguise and the confirmation of Christ's divine power.

I think this is also the fundamental message of the angel's message to Benjamin: You will know you have found the true king when you discover him in the most unexpected place. Benjamin's angel does not mention the swaddling clothes or the manger, but he points toward a place that, from some perspectives, is almost as unexpected. The Lord Omnipotent will dwell in a tabernacle of clay. He will be found in a human body that, fragile as clay, is subject to decay and damage. The manger and the swaddling clothes protect a body of flesh subject to the same fatigue and pain that Benjamin himself knows. One can imagine that Benjamin wants to ask: "How can a perishable body like mine be the place of divine omnipotence?" That tender body is both the disguise and the confirmation of Christ's divine power. *And this shall be a sign unto you; ye shall find the Lord wrapped in flesh, pulsing with blood and breath.*

Christ's power is an important theme in Benjamin's gospel, in hand with the vulnerability of his body. I think this power, too, would have been displayed to the people in the condition of Benjamin's aged body. After all, Benjamin once wielded the sword of Laban with the strength of his arm and established peace among his people with the force of his frame (Words of Mormon 1:13). Those great works are now written on his person, disguised and confirmed by the carved landscape of his flesh. In this way, in presenting Christ's great power as a central theme of his life, Benjamin's gospel stands apart from Mary's. Mary is a young mother; Benjamin is an aged king. Both are shown the Savior in images and conditions that resonate in their own lives. Where Mary holds the son of God, a vulnerable infant, in her arms, Mosiah speaks of "the Lord Omnipotent who reigneth, who was, and is from all eternity to all eternity" (Mosiah 3:5). This striking title, the Lord Omnipotent, is repeated four times in this passage. Where Mary's perspective focuses on the *con* in "condescension," Christ's life in solidarity with fragile mortals like you and me, Benjamin's focuses on the *descent*, the power and might that Christ brings down from heaven to earth. He uses this power to bless ordinary men and women, "working mighty miracles" among them (Mosiah 3:5).

But if this Savior, this Lord Omnipotent, comes bearing superlative power, that power is twinned with equally superlative suffering: "And lo, he shall suffer . . . even more than man can suffer, except it be unto death" (Mosiah 3:7). The way King Benjamin makes this point struck me as amusing the first time I read it, or at least ironic, as if Benjamin were trying a little too hard to convince his people of Christ's preeminence: "The Lord who is coming is so great that even in abject suffering he's superhuman!" Isn't superhuman abjection a nonsensical contradiction? But I was brought up short by lines from another gospel. In Matthew's account of the Crucifixion, passersby who witnessed Christ's suffering reacted with mocking irony: "Thou that destroyest the temple, and buildest it in three days, save thyself. If thou be the Son of God, come down from the cross" (Matthew 27:40). They assumed that suffering is incompatible with divinity: "If you're really God's son, prove it by saving yourself!" Likewise, my amused response to Benjamin's image was based on the assumption that divine omnipotence would avert suffering and humiliation precisely as confirmation of its power.

In fact, the message of Benjamin's gospel seems to be just the opposite: the power of the Lord Omnipotent, the Father and Creator of heaven and earth, is linked with the extremity of his suffering. With this link in mind, I started to feel a heartbeat pulsing through Benjamin's gospel, a two-beat rhythm on notes of power and weakness. Christ is the reigning Lord Omnipotent, who was and is from all eternity to all eternity. And yet he shall dwell in a tabernacle of clay, a human body fashioned from the perishable matter of this world (Mosiah 3:5). Christ will work mighty miracles, showing forth divine power as he heals the sick, raises the dead, and cures the lame, the blind, the deaf, and the tormented. And yet he himself will suffer extreme temptation, pain, hunger, thirst, fatigue, and anguish, to the point of weeping blood through his very skin (Mosiah 3:7). Christ will bear the exalted titles of the Son of God, the Father of heaven and earth, and the Creator of all things from the beginning. And yet he will also be the son of Mary, and through her human body and nurture he will make his life among the human family he calls "his own" (Mosiah 3:8–9). The name of Christ can sustain a faith sufficiently powerful to save the human family. And yet the person of Christ will be misjudged, condemned, tortured, and crucified (Mosiah 3:9).

Benjamin's phrase "even after all this" captures the contrast that he is trying to build, I think (Mosiah 3:9). Christ is the Lord

Omnipotent, the Son of God, the Creator come down from heaven with miraculous powers to bless and heal and save the world. But even after all this, he assumes a human body born to a human mother. Even after all this, he suffers and dies. "Even after all this they shall consider him a man" (Mosiah 3:9). It's as though the people witness Christ's evident vulnerability and reason backward, concluding that he couldn't possibly be a God, couldn't possibly have come down from heaven. This is the root of Christ's hiddenness in the world, the reason why angels—whether in Bethlehem or Zarahemla—are necessary to tell us where and how to find the Savior. The reality of his human suffering becomes a kind of disguise, the manger and swaddling clothes hiding the truth of his power and the wonder of his miraculous works. Where do we find Christ? *And this shall be a sign unto you.*

How could they have been blind to the signs and wonders of his power, even after all the miraculous healings and the raising of the dead? This is the central question of Benjamin's gospel, and it's the question he puts urgently to us. Will we, too, find ourselves Christ-blind in the world? Will we be misled by the disguise of suffering? When confronted with the ugliness of extreme misery, don't we often respond in the same way—with scorn, judgment, and revulsion instead of compassion? Don't we scramble to produce an explanation for the suffering, seizing on anything that allows us to believe that only the weak and guilty can suffer so? I think this flawed, familiar logic is at the center of the self-deceptive judgment that blinds the people to Christ's power. And Benjamin returns to precisely this same interplay of self-deception and judgment when he warns his people, later in his speech, against condemning the beggar in his misery. "Perhaps thou shalt say: The man has brought upon himself his misery; therefore I will stay my hand . . . for his punishments are just—but I say unto you, O man, whosoever doeth this the same hath great cause to repent" (Mosiah 4:17–18). Benjamin's gospel shows that the mistaken reasoning employed by the world to condemn Christ is identical to that used by the self-righteous to condemn the beggar. The beggar's misery is wrongly used to prove his guilt.

This is something you've written about, Adam, and that we've talked about together before. In your book *Original Grace,* you show that Benjamin's discussion of the beggar teaches us how to exercise justice as God does, in love and without assuming that a person's suffering is deserved.[6] As I've studied the angel's retelling of Christ's life on the night before Benjamin delivers that sermon, it has struck me that the angel is implicitly teaching the same lesson. We see how Christ's misery is wrongly used to deny his divinity, just as the beggar's misery is wrongly used to deny his claim on us (Mosiah 3:7–9; compare Mosiah 4:17). Both figures, the Savior and the beggar, are wrapped in a ragged cloak of suffering that, for the Christ-blind, disguises the essential nature they share as beggar and Lord. Christ came to his people in a body, the site of their own suffering, and for that they considered him a man and condemned him as they would a beggar.

This point raises a final question for me. Are the people right or wrong to consider Christ a man? And how are we to find Christ in the world, if he comes among us in man-disguise? Benjamin makes it clear that they are wrong to consider him *just* a man: he is the Lord Omnipotent and the Father of heaven and earth. But in the end they aren't wrong, I think, to consider him a man. Their backward-judging logic is profoundly flawed, yet their conclusion is sound: Jesus Christ is a man, though both his power and his suffering are greater than all men's. The heartbeat that propels this gospel, that pulsing interplay between Christ's power and Christ's vulnerability, makes that clear. He is a man. And for the Christ-eyed, his cloak of flesh is not a disguise but a message: "that ye may learn that when ye are in the service of your fellow beings ye are only in the service of your God" (Mosiah 2:17).

This is his sign to us: we find him wherever our fellow beings are cloaked in suffering, wherever they mourn and stand in need of comfort. He walks among us in a body of flesh. His heart beats and ceases beating at a terrible cost. And our salvation was, and is, and is to come, in the flux of that rushing blood.

Rosalynde

"For the natural man is an enemy to God, and has been from the fall of Adam, and will be, forever and ever, unless he yields to the enticings of the Holy Spirit, and putteth off the natural man and becometh a saint through the atonement of Christ the Lord, and becometh as a child, submissive, meek, humble, patient, full of love, willing to submit to all things which the Lord seeth fit to inflict upon him, even as a child doth submit to his father." (Mosiah 3:19)

Rosalynde,

You're right to say that this chapter has a strong pulse. And you're right, I think, to nonetheless recognize that this beating heart belongs to a grizzled man who's "waxed old," worn himself out in the service of his God, and knows that, as nature demands, "he must very soon go the way of all the earth" (Mosiah 1:9).

Both this chapter and 1 Nephi 11, as you note, turn on revelations delivered by angels. But where it's easy to imagine a young Nephi staying up all night, unable to sleep as he "sat pondering" on his father's words, Benjamin himself tells us that he was woken *from* sleep by the angel's repeated command, "Awake . . . . Awake, and hear the words which I shall tell thee" (1 Nephi 11:1; Mosiah 3:2, 3). And where Nephi is carried off "into an exceedingly high mountain" and granted a sweeping vision of global salvation history, Benjamin is only asked to sit on the edge of his bed and hear—not see—the angel's much more local message about how a "natural man," despite being an enemy to God, can still be saved.

In this sense, I think it's helpful to suggest that where 1 Nephi 11 is about mothers and babies, Mosiah 3 is about old men. Benjamin's gospel is backlit by death.

This, I think, also fits with a general shift in angelic vocabulary. Here, the previous angel's insistent (and unusual) emphasis on "condescension" disappears entirely. Instead, one word stands out to me in Mosiah 3, a word that never appears in 1 Nephi 11: *blood.*

Benjamin's angel mentions "blood" five times in just twenty-seven verses.

In Mosiah 3:7, the angel introduces the subject of blood when he reports that Christ "shall suffer temptations, and pain of body, hunger, thirst, and fatigue, even more than man can suffer, except it be unto death; for behold, blood cometh from every pore, so great shall be his anguish for the wickedness and the abominations of his people." And then, returning to this image again and again, the angel repeats that this blood matters because it *atones*. In verse 11 he says, "His blood atoneth"; in verse 15, "The atonement of his blood"; in verse 16, "The blood of Christ atoneth"; and in verse 18 he concludes, "Salvation was, and is, and is to come, in and through the atoning blood of Christ, the Lord Omnipotent."

What is blood? How does it save and atone? And how does this atoning blood connect to the two-beat rhythm of power and weakness you identified as this chapter's pulse?

Again, let me suggest just one reading from among many.

In the Old Testament, religion centers on blood. To worship God is to offer acceptable sacrifices and to offer acceptable sacrifices is to shed blood. As Leviticus 17 explains, atoning sacrifices require blood because "the life of the flesh is in the blood" (Leviticus 17:11).

What is blood? Blood is life. Blood is life in liquid, concentrated form. And, specifically, blood is the life of the mortal body's flesh. "The life of all flesh is the blood thereof" (Leviticus 17:14).

Tellingly, Leviticus 17 equates life and blood in the context of two intertwined commandments: (1) the commandment that, to be eaten, flesh must first be drained of its blood because "no soul of you shall eat blood," and (2) the commandment that, to be properly sacrificed, the animal's blood must be shed "upon the altar to make an atonement for your souls: for it is the blood that maketh an atonement for the soul" (Leviticus 17:12, 11).

While flesh may be eaten, the blood may not. The blood—the life of the flesh—belongs exclusively to God.

As Leviticus has it, life's blood never belongs to the devoured or the devourer. Even if my flesh is in some sense my own, the life that circulates through that flesh is not. That life is always given, always borrowed, and must always be returned. And as a result, beyond anything I can claim or control, the life pumping through my veins always has a life of its own, a life that belongs to God, not me.

This is true, I think, in a very literal way.

I try, most mornings, to pray. And, most mornings, I try to give most of that time to listening rather than talking. And on those mornings when a seed of silence blossoms into something like a quiet mind, the first thing that comes into focus is my flesh, lit up with a kind of interior light: my body, my posture, the weight of my head, the tension in my back, the pressure in my gut, my lungs expanding and contracting—and then there, back behind the more obvious ebb and flow of my breath, is the steady beating of my heart and the subtle roar of blood in my ears. I can feel, directly and immediately, the life pounding through me, the blood looped through my fingers and toes, and I'm surprised, every time, by how little any of it has to do with me. Rarely, and only with real effort, do I know anything about my own heart.

My heart beats and my blood pumps with a life all their own. I can't command it or control it. And though my body would die without it, the life in that flesh doesn't belong to me. The life in that flesh belongs to God. The life in that flesh is his to give and his to take.

Something both liberating and empowering tends to follow from noticing and acknowledging this basic fact of life: that my heart beats without me, that my blood is indifferent to me, that my life doesn't belong to me.

Which brings us back to death—and, ultimately, to sacrifice.

It's possible to lose our lives—it's possible to die—because our lives are not our own. Blood gives flesh its life. And, in turn, the shedding of blood typifies what allows the flesh to die. Because blood is the stuff of life, it's also the stuff of death. With blood, only a knife's edge separates one from the other, dividing life from death.

In Mosiah 3, blood seems to be crucial for this same reason: blood is how life crosses over into death, and thus, Christ's lifeblood is what allows him—the Lord Omnipotent—not only to die but to put his own divine twist on death. It's what allows Christ to die in the specific way that simultaneously *atones*. It's what allows Christ to undergo his own death as a willing sacrifice.

More on this in a moment.

First, let me circle back to note that all this talk of blood—and especially of atoning blood, of blood that's been shed—fits the mood of Mosiah 3, staged as it is in the shadow of Benjamin's coming death. And, what's more, I'd also suggest that all this talk of blood goes hand in hand with the angel's other key innovation in Benjamin's gospel vocabulary: the angel's famous explanation of what it means to be a "natural man" (Mosiah 3:19).

Given how familiar this phrase has become, I didn't expect to learn that this formula is only used six times in our scriptures. It's used twice, and most memorably, in Mosiah 3:19. Apart from that, it's only used one other time in the Book of Mormon, once in the Doctrine and Covenants, and once in Moses (Alma 26:21; Doctrine and Covenants 67:12; Moses 1:14).

The other use belongs to Paul in 1 Corinthians 2:14. And this is where Joseph Smith, our inspired translator, would have heard it first.

In 1 Corinthian 2:14, Paul says, "But the natural man receiveth not the things of the Spirit of God: for they are foolishness unto him: neither can he know them, because they are spiritually discerned."

The King James Version's "natural man" renders Paul's *psychikos anthropos*, where *anthropos* means "human" and *psychikos* means "breath of life" or "the principle of life which humans have in common with animals." The natural man is the fleshy, animal dimension of a human being.

But later in this same letter Paul tweaks this formula, changing the term from "natural man" to "natural body." And here, I think, Paul's meaning is even clearer. Describing the resurrection of the dead, Paul says that the human body "is sown in corruption; it is raised in incorruption: . . . It is sown a natural body; it is raised a spiritual body" (1 Corinthians 15:42, 44).

What is a "natural" body? It's a body sown in corruption. It's the human body subject to a natural, inevitable corruption and dissolution. The natural body is the mortal body, the body that depends on blood, the body that's naturally going to die and that will need to be resurrected.

Or, simply: the natural man is the dying man.

This is why "the natural man is an enemy to God, and has been from the fall of Adam" (Mosiah 3:19). The natural man is an enemy to God because the Fall introduced death and the natural man *doesn't want to die.*

The natural body is afraid to die.

The fundamental problem is fear.

And this primal fear, it seems to me, is the root reason why the natural man refuses to yield to the Spirit and become like "a child, submissive, meek, humble, patient, full of love, willing to submit to all things which the Lord seeth fit to inflict upon him" (Mosiah 3:19). The Lord sees fit to have the natural body be mortal. And beyond all mortality's other troubles, the Lord sees fit "to inflict" death upon those natural bodies and, thus, claim those bodies as his own.

Faced with death—faced with the fact that the life of all flesh is in the blood and that this blood belongs, not to them, but to God—the natural body refuses to yield. Afraid, it refuses to submit. It refuses to concede. Filled with fear, natural bodies become enemies to God as they try to wrestle their life's blood away from God, as they try to claim their lives as their own, control their own fate, and avoid death altogether.

This is what it means to be a sinner. Sinners live as if their life's blood belonged to them. They live life on the run from God, terrified to yield to his will. Running from God, the natural body "doth . . . shrink from the presence of the Lord into a state of misery," and in this way, they all "have drunk damnation to their own souls" (Mosiah 3:25).

Instead of giving their life's blood back to God by way of sacrifice, sinners try to keep those lives for themselves.

We can yield our lives to God and be filled with *his* life. Or we can claim our lives as our *own* and be cut off from his life. But there's no third path.

How, then, might blood atone rather than damn?

As always, Jesus shows the way. His willingness to shed his blood on eternity's altar—his willingness to suffer "more than man can suffer" and bleed from every pore—enables him to transfigure death into sacrifice (Mosiah 3:7).

By shedding his life's blood, he gives his life back to God. By losing his life, he saves his life and ours. He atones for us by changing fear into love and, thus, death into a loving sacrifice.

And this sacrifice, in turn, opens the same path to us.

Embraced by his love, we're empowered to put aside our fears and trust his sacrifice by offering our own. Empowered by his love, we learn how to finally "yield to the enticings of the Holy Spirit" and become like "a child, submissive, meek, humble, patient, full of love" (Mosiah 3:19).

Children are the model, here, for the same reason as the elderly. Those who are very young, just like those who are very old, can't sustain the sinful fantasy that their lives are their own, that their bodies are their own, that their blood is their own. And that fantasy's impossibility is what fits them for faith and humility and trusting sacrifice. It's what fits them for redemption.

And this, I think, is just a variation on that same two-stroke heartbeat of divine power and divine weakness you identified as the pulse of this chapter. Christ's power to save is a product of his power to submit. He's able to save our lives because he yields to the necessity of losing his own life. He's able to overcome death and conquer fear through willing sacrifice. And, like your grandpa, this willingness to yield to God's claim on his life is irrevocably engraved in his hands.

Adam

— CHAPTER 3 —

The Gospel of Abinadi

MOSIAH 15

Captured and carried in chains before the court of King Noah, the prophet Abinadi proclaims that salvation comes through the Messiah, who is the fulfillment of the law of Moses. Abinadi recites Isaiah's great poem of the suffering servant, a man of sorrows who has borne our griefs. Abinadi then interprets the meaning of the scripture, declaring that God himself will come down among the children of men. Abinadi teaches that Jesus Christ, the incarnate God, is both Father and Son in the relation of his spirit to his flesh. Abinadi prophesies that Christ will suffer temptation of body and disownment by his people, but he will not yield. He will go silently to his death, like a sheep to the slaughter, making his will subject to the Father and his flesh subject to crucifixion. Filled with the bowels of mercy, Abinadi teaches, Christ will break the bands of death and redeem his people.

"And after all this, after working many mighty miracles among the children of men, he shall be led, yea, even as Isaiah said, as a sheep before the shearer is dumb, so he opened not his mouth. Yea, even so he shall be led, crucified, and slain, the flesh becoming subject even unto death, the will of the Son being swallowed up in the will of the Father." (Mosiah 15:6–7)

Adam,

You and I are about the same age, trekking that long, featureless steppe of adulthood between the blue hills of young parenthood on one side and the rough country of old age on the other. On a map, we'd be somewhere between Mary, the virgin mother, and Benjamin, the gray king. I celebrated my birthday last week by climbing a big mountain with my son. He set a vigorous pace, and my legs followed obediently, my heart galloping along to see the sun rise over the hills and steppe and rough country spread out below. I am able-bodied, of sound mind, and unaccountably lucky, for as long or short as this unearned state of affairs might hold out. But as I climbed my birthday mountain, I also kept checking my phone for updates from a friend's deathbed.

You're right that this luck, this obedient, galloping body of mine, is also a kind of loss. It's a loss because I am losing it, to age and everything else, sunrise by sunrise. But there's something else lost. Like you say, the infant, the old, and the ill know something that's lost on us vigorous steppe climbers: they know the twin truths of our mortality and our dependence. They know what it is to be preserved from day to day, lent breath, supported from one moment to another (see Mosiah 2:21). And they know the darker side of that truth: they know wretchedness; they know humiliation.

I have always been in the camp of "do not go gentle into that good night." Or better, the camp of "I am not resigned to the shutting away of loving hearts in the hard ground." And why not? Life is good. Its blue hills, its long steppes, its rough country. "Lovers and thinkers, into the earth with you." I will rage vainly at that deathbed. I will shake my fist at the death that rests in the belly of life. "Crowned / With lilies and with laurel they go; but I am not resigned." I know that what you say about the lifeblood that pumps through Benjamin's gospel is true: either I give life away, or I watch it taken against my will. "I know. But I do not approve. And I am not resigned."[7]

Maybe I just want to howl on the road to the altar where, in the end, I will offer up a consecrated life. I think Job would understand me, a fellow howler (see Job 3:3–26). But I suspect Abinadi might not.

Abinadi is a prophet's prophet: eccentric, incorrigible, constantly spouting difficult poetry. He preaches a bracing gospel, with no time to coddle my resistance or rage. Compared to Benjamin, the beloved servant-leader, Abinadi is alien and fierce. Where Benjamin's gospel is delivered simply and directly from his iconic tower, Abinadi's gospel is declared in a setting that is busy with intrigue and drama. After dropping a string of blistering condemnations among the revanchist people of Zeniff, the unknown Abinadi, having come in disguise, is apprehended, bound, and brought before an apostate priesthood (Mosiah 12:9, 17). There the prophet accuses Noah's priests of violating the law of Moses and corrupting its meaning (Mosiah 12:29). With the words of Moses on his tongue and "exceeding luster" in his face, "even as Moses," Abinadi recreates something of the Sinai experience in the midst of the corrupt court (Mosiah 13:5). He then links the Law with the Prophets, quoting

Isaiah at length to show that the law has always pointed to its own fulfillment in God's saving love (see Mosiah 14; Mosiah 13:33–35). Isaiah's prophetic poem about the suffering servant, a "man of sorrows, and acquainted with grief," is no easier for Noah's priests to understand than it is for modern readers, and so Abinadi undertakes to interpret the meaning of the prophecy. It is through interpretation of poetry, then, after reprising the Law and the Prophets and reviewing the Bible from Exodus to Isaiah, that Abinadi finally arrives at his gospel: "I would that ye should understand that God himself shall come down among the children of men, and shall redeem his people" (Mosiah 15:1).

Just as Benjamin's gospel depicts the life of Jesus Christ in terms that resonate with Benjamin's own experience, Abinadi bears a resemblance to the Redeemer of his gospel. Christ, like Abinadi, comes in disguise. Jesus takes upon him a body of flesh with "no form nor comeliness . . . [nor] beauty that we should desire him," which hinders the people from understanding his full identity as God himself (Mosiah 14:2). Like Abinadi, the unknown Christ manifests miraculous power with and in his human body. Both are bound, scourged, and led before a hostile tribunal. And both are delivered up to "suffer even until death" (Mosiah 17:10). One role of a prophet is to stand in for God as a surrogate before his people, and Abinadi seals his surrogacy with his own life.

There's one way in which Abinadi differs dramatically from the Son introduced in his gospel. Abinadi is a talker. He is a prodigious orator, quoting long passages of scripture and extemporaneously interpreting and proclaiming "the message which the Lord sent [him] to deliver" (Mosiah 13:3). In total, Abinadi's preaching makes up all or most of seven continuous chapters in the book of Mosiah (chapters 11–17). His oral performance is remarkable by any standard. And so it is notable that, of all the rich images available in Isaiah to describe the Son of God, Abinadi chooses to highlight this one: Christ's silence. "And after all this, after working many mighty miracles among the children of men, he shall be led, yea, even as Isaiah said, as a sheep before the shearer is dumb, so he opened not his mouth" (Mosiah 15:6). In light of Abinadi's effusive eloquence up until the very moment of martyrdom, Christ's silence before death's blade is devastating.

What are we to make of this divine silence? Ironically, this is one subject Abinadi doesn't enlarge. A thousand answers could be piled on, despite the futility of jangling words in the face of God's stillness. No doubt the best way to understand Christ's silence is to practice it oneself, as you do most mornings, Adam: listening. But laboring as we must under the tiresome tradition that books should contain words, I'll hazard a suggestion where Abinadi offers none. As we've seen, Abinadi draws on the imagery in Isaiah 53, the song of a suffering servant whom Abinadi relates to the Son of God. Christ is described as a sheep bound for slaughter, unresisting and silent before death. It's an image that calls back both to Nephi's vision of the Lamb of God, slain for the sins of the world, and to Benjamin's vision of the exhausted, bleeding Lord. Abinadi adds another dimension to this layered portrait: he dwells on Christ's passivity. The sheep's silence is a symbol of its submission and powerlessness. Christ's stillness is, among other things, an aspect of his passive acceptance of others' actions along the road to crucifixion. He displays no active resistance to the people's maltreatment, but "suffereth himself to be mocked, and scourged, and cast out, and disowned by his people" (Mosiah 15:5). He "was oppressed, and he was afflicted, yet he opened not his mouth" (Mosiah 14:7).

To clarify what is particular about Abinadi's gospel, consider two meanings of the word *suffer*. This is a key word in Benjamin's description of Christ's mortal experience: "And lo, he shall suffer temptations, and pain of body, hunger, thirst, and fatigue, even more than man can suffer, except it be unto death" (Mosiah 3:7).

Here Benjamin uses the word as we typically use it: to endure pain, distress, injury, or misery. Christ, by virtue of his mortal body, experienced the same pain and anguish that we do. We've seen why that point is important to Benjamin. But Abinadi uses the word *suffer* in a different way: Christ "suffereth temptation, and yieldeth not to the temptation, but suffereth himself to be mocked, and scourged, and cast out, and disowned by his people" (Mosiah 15:5). Here, to *suffer* means to allow, to tolerate, or to be subject to something. Christ is subject to temptation and allows himself to be mocked and disowned without resistance. He is passive, open, accepting of all that the world gives. He is affected by and available to the world he has entered; he drinks the bitter cup and bears the bruises of iniquity. He suffers the world.

With this understanding of Christ's suffering in mind, Abinadi's gospel seems to become an exploration of divine meekness. After his stunning opening line—"God himself will come down among the children of men, and shall redeem his people"—he launches into a difficult passage on the way that Jesus Christ, as God himself, is both Father and Son. Abinadi dwells on the internal relation of these two aspects of his person.

One way to cut through the difficult construction of Abinadi's gospel is to look for the thread of the Son's meekness woven throughout. The Son of God, in his fleshly guise, is "subject" to—that is, dependent upon and obedient to—the Father. The Son's will is submissive to the Father's will. The Son appears mostly in passive grammatical forms: he is mocked, scourged, led, cast out, disowned, crucified, slain. He is subject to death and remains silent and passive in its shadow, as we've seen. This is the Christ of Philippians 2, the Son who "took upon him the form of a servant, and was made in the likeness of men: and being found in fashion as a man, he humbled himself, and became obedient unto death, even the death of the cross" (Philippians 2:7–8).

For me, the most resonant expression of the Son's passivity is the image of his being swallowed: "the will of the Son [is] swallowed up in the will of the Father" as he submits his life-clinging flesh to death (Mosiah 15:7). I love the way this image has echoes of Christ's words of submission in the Garden of Gethsemane, which he expresses as an act of swallowing: "O my Father, if this cup may not pass away from me, except I drink it, thy will be done" (Matthew 26:42). Christ swallows a bitter death, suffering (or allowing) his will to be swallowed by the Father just as his body will be swallowed by the tomb. And in swallowing death by crucifixion, all the pain and humiliation—the other kind of suffering—fill his bowels with mercy. Death always rests in the belly of life.

But from that dark cradle, Christ's death transforms life from within. Christ's stillness at the cross is what enables his death—powerfully, magnificently—to break the bonds of death. As you put it, Adam, Christ's *way of dying* puts a divine twist on death, allowing him to die in a way that reconciles with life. And so it's not at all coincidental that Abinadi's description of Christ's willing passivity so closely matches Benjamin's description of what it's like to be saved in Christ. As Benjamin describes it, salvation is what happens when the natural man "becometh a saint through the atonement of Christ the Lord, and becometh as a child, submissive, meek, humble, patient, full of love, willing to submit to all things which the Lord seeth fit to inflict upon him, even as a child doth submit to his father" (Mosiah 3:19). It's as if Abinadi shaped his portrait of Christ around Benjamin's theology of salvation. In Abinadi's gospel, Christ is drawn as a *saint*—submissive, meek, humble, patient, willing to submit the flesh of the Son to the spirit of the Father.

Which brings me to a final point, bookmarked here for our further exploration in later chapters: Book of Mormon gospels are preludes (or occasionally postludes) to sermons on salvation. The lives of Christ we receive from the Book of Mormon do not work in the text as historical accounts or theological raw materials, as they do in the New Testament gospels. Instead, Book of Mormon prophets offer their gospels as illustrations, expressions, or explanations of the redemption offered to the reader through Christ's atonement. Just as each prophet shapes his portrait of the Savior in different ways, so each sermon on salvation is organized around a different aspect of our return to the presence of God. But the intent is always the same: to provoke our faith, to transform our hearts, to teach us a better way of dying and rising in Christ.

Abinadi shows me that better way, urging me to swallow my howls. Or, failing that, teaching me not to let my howls swallow me.

Rosalynde

"And thus God breaketh the bands of death." (Mosiah 15:8)

Rosalynde,

I'm sorry for your friend's passing. I'm sorry for her, for her family, and for you. There's nothing wrong with anger or grief in the face of death—I am, in fact, cheered at the thought of you raging against loving hearts (my own included) being shut away in the ground—but in the face of these strong emotions, the critical question is always the same: how do we redeem them? How do we avoid being destroyed by them? How do we repurpose their strength in the service of life and creation?

Abinadi, especially as a type of Christ, may be just the tutor we need.

Adding Abinadi now to Mary (and Nephi) and Benjamin, the layers of lives and gospels are beginning to add up. Our text is getting thick. Common themes are easier to see, and variations stand out more sharply. It's becoming easier to see how the same Christ is revealed in these many different lives.

We have Mary's experience of God's love and condescension wrapped inside of Nephi's global vision of Israel's collective redemption.

We have Benjamin's localized angelic message about how a natural man can become a saint through the blood of Christ, projected against the backdrop of his own impending death.

And now we have Abinadi's dense account of how "God himself shall come down among the children of men, and shall redeem his people," an account that boldly explains this divine incarnation in terms of Christ bearing within himself both "the Father" and "the Son" (Mosiah 15:1)—and an account that, in maximally dramatic fashion, is delivered as Abinadi stands trial for his life.

In this respect, Abinadi is indeed a prophet's prophet. He's much more like a classic Old Testament prophet than Nephi or Benjamin. Rather than being a king, Abinadi is an outsider. He is, as you say, eccentric and incorrigible. He's alien and fierce. He appears to blow in from nowhere, a nobody, without power or reputation, crying repentance and prophesying destruction. He's hunted for two years until he reappears to seal his testimony. And where Nephi and Benjamin both report stunning revelations delivered by angels, Abinadi's final message is shaped by an interpretive contest with Noah's priests, a contest that turns on who, at the end of the day, can actually read and understand Isaiah.

This, I think, is a point worth emphasizing again. In Mosiah 15, Abinadi's gospel isn't delivered by an angel. Abinadi's gospel comes in the form of an impromptu—and inspired and messianic—reading of Isaiah's poetry.

We shouldn't play favorites with prophets, but I love everything about Abinadi. I love that he's not someone special or important or powerful. I love that he doesn't care one whit about Noah's anger or threats. I love that he ultimately finds his clearest prophetic voice by interpreting poetry. And I love that in the process, almost as a sidebar, he *also* happens to deliver what may be the richest and deepest account of Christ's incarnation in all of scripture—better, even, than John 1 or Doctrine and Covenants 93.

If you exiled me to a desert island and said I could take only one chapter of scripture, I'd think hard about packing Mosiah 15.

This wasn't always obvious to me, but a few years ago I spent the better part of a summer reading and rereading this chapter. You'll know what I'm talking about. For almost fifteen years now you and I have been involved in a scholarly project—the Latter-day Saint

Theology Seminar—that's dedicated to generating close readings of Restoration scripture. In many ways, we owe our friendship to this shared work.

This shared affinity for close readings of scripture won't be lost on our readers. By now, they'll surely have noticed that you and I, rather than treating scripture like a black box meant only to be admired from a safe distance or taken out only on special occasions, treat it more like a classic car engine that invites readers to get their hands dirty, take it apart, see how it works, and assemble it again.

And this, of course, is the kind of work we must do. If we really want to understand how the engine works, we have to take it apart bolt by bolt, spark plug by spark plug, and put it back together again. And again. And then, as we do this work, the work rebuilds us.

The theology seminar is like a lab for taking blocks of scripture apart and putting them back together again, sentence by sentence, phrase by phrase, word by word. Its method is unusual but straightforward: take eight scholars with different kinds of expertise, half men and half women, and lock them in a room for two weeks with just twenty verses of scripture. Meet for five hours a day, focus on just two or three verses, eat something, and spend another five hours preparing to meet again the next day. From as many angles as possible—theological, philosophical, historical, psychological, sociological, political, rhetorical, etc.—strip each verse down to its raw, component pieces and then try to map out, idea by idea, something like an exploded-view diagram that labels all the parts and suspends each screw in line with its threaded slot.

The experience is beautiful, intense, painstaking, and exhausting. Few people are likely to envy us the grunt work of scrutinizing punctuation, diagramming sentences, tracing arguments, and tracking down intertextual allusions for ten hours a day, but I've grown to love it.

A few years ago, we were both part of a seminar like this. The eight of us lived for two weeks in a sort of monastery, far from home, sleeping in tiny, wood-paneled cells on narrow beds. In addition to the bed, each room had a small wooden desk. We met every day in an unused classroom. We shoved most of the desks against the wall and circled the rest in the center of the room. That year, our block of text was from Mosiah 4.

But a few years before this, I'd done the same work with a seminar dedicated to reading Mosiah 15. Looking back on that collaborative work, two things stand out to me now: how Mosiah 15 is really an explanation of Isaiah and how the chapter's famously difficult (and never quite grammatical) opening verses are better read as an explanation of Christ's atonement than the Godhead's nature.

The verses at the heart of Abinadi's trial are Isaiah 52:7–10. These are the verses that Noah's wicked priests challenge Abinadi to interpret as "they began to question him, that they might cross him, that thereby they might have wherewith to accuse him" (Mosiah 12:19). Quoting Isaiah 52:7–10 in Mosiah 12:21–24, the priests ask Abinadi point blank: "What meaneth the words which are written, and which have been taught by our fathers?" (Mosiah 12:20).

For our purposes here, let's use a clean, modern translation of those same verses as quoted by Noah's priests:

> How beautiful upon the mountains
>   are the feet of the messenger who announces peace,
> who brings good news,
>   who announces salvation,
>   who says to Zion, "Your God reigns."
> Listen! Your sentinels lift up their voices;
>   together they shout for joy,
> for in plain sight they see
>   the return of the Lord to Zion.

> Break forth; shout together for joy,
> you ruins of Jerusalem;
> for the Lord has comforted his people;
> he has redeemed Jerusalem.
> The Lord has bared his holy arm
> before the eyes of all the nations,
> and all the ends of the earth shall see
> the salvation of our God.
> (Isaiah 52:7–10, NRSV)

These are powerful and compelling verses. But the crucial question is why Noah's *priests* care about these particular verses—verses about God's people triumphantly returning to their promised land, to Zion—in the first place.

These chapters in Mosiah hint at the reason without ever quite saying. But I think our friend Joseph Spencer persuasively connects the dots.

Spencer suggests that, in context, these verses are most likely important to Noah's people because they see *themselves* as fulfilling this prophecy. In their eyes, these verses are about them.[8]

By leaving Zarahemla and returning to settle again in the land of Nephi—that is, by returning to the land originally promised to their fathers, the land now occupied by Lamanites—they have returned from exile to reclaim and redeem Zion and, thus, can rightly and joyfully proclaim "the return of the Lord to Zion" (Isaiah 52:8, NRSV). And by restoring them to this promised land, "the Lord hath comforted his people" (Isaiah 52:9). As Limhi explains it to Ammon: "I am Limhi, the son of Noah, who was the son of Zeniff, who came up out of the land of Zarahemla to inherit this land, which was the land of their fathers" (Mosiah 7:9).

It seems reasonable, then, to assume that these verses from Isaiah 52 have functioned as something like this people's national anthem, the keystone of their self-understanding as God's redeemed and chosen people. And by challenging Abinadi to interpret exactly these verses, Noah's priests are daring him to publicly contradict—in a court of law, to the king's own face—the fulfillment of this cherished prophecy with his sour predictions of the people's impending destruction.

Abinadi, though, doesn't fall into their trap. Rather, he applies a bit of theological jujitsu and reclaims these verses on behalf of the *true* messiah who will redeem Zion, the true messiah who will announce peace and salvation and declare that God does in fact now reign over all nations. Abinadi reclaims these verses by pushing beyond their narrow, self-congratulatory application to Noah's people and widening their scope to include "the eyes of all the nations" and "all the ends of the earth" (Isaiah 52:10).

To Noah's wicked priests, Abinadi's rebuttal is simple: Noah's kingdom isn't God's kingdom. Only God's reign is God's reign. And God won't personally reign in Zion until after "God himself shall come down among the children of men, and shall redeem his people" (Mosiah 15:1).

The whole of Abinadi's sermon, weaving all the way from Mosiah 12 through Mosiah 16, is ultimately aimed at the reclamation of those verses from Isaiah 52. And the climax of that sermon in Mosiah 15—coming as it does only after he has reprised the Law and the Prophets and reviewed the Bible from Exodus to Isaiah—reveals their true meaning by explicitly knotting the triumphant prophecy of Isaiah 52 together with the much more difficult song that follows hard on its heels in Isaiah 53: Isaiah's rightly celebrated Song of the Suffering Servant (compare Mosiah 14).

By tying Isaiah 52 (compare Mosiah 15:14–31) to Isaiah 53 (compare Mosiah 15:1–13), Abinadi is effectively saying: here, Noah, is what a *real* king looks like. Here is what it looks like when God himself reigns: it looks like the greatest of all becoming the servant of all.

God's reign looks like a servant willing to suffer for his people. It looks like "a man of sorrows," a man "acquainted with grief," a man who has surely "borne our griefs, and carried our sorrows; yet we did esteem him stricken, smitten of God, and afflicted. But he was wounded for our transgressions, he was bruised for our iniquities; the chastisement of our peace was upon him; and with his stripes we are healed" (Mosiah 14:3, 4–5; compare Isaiah 53:3, 4–5).

This is the great messianic secret.

And this chapter—Isaiah 53—is the messianic linchpin of the entire Old Testament.

We've come, then, full circle to the root question of anger and grief and how to redeem them. And we've come, at the same time, back to your skillful reading of how Mosiah 15 turns on questions about the redemptive nature of divine silence, divine suffering, and divine passivity.

I think we can agree that there is nothing inherently redemptive about silence, suffering, and passivity. Pain, by itself, is just pain. Rather, what we need are *divine* modes of silence, *divine* modes of suffering, and *divine* modes of passivity. We need to understand how, in God's hands, these things can be consecrated and redeemed.

And this, you'll recall, was the second point I took away from the summer I spent rereading Mosiah 15: that verses 1–8 are better read as a description of how Christ, in himself, redeems grief and sorrow, and not as a muddled description of what Latter-day Saints believe about the Godhead.

Abinadi, of course, never claims to be speaking about the Godhead. Instead, he's busy explaining why Isaiah 53 is the key to understanding Isaiah 52. Granted, that explanation is compact and unusual, and in the process, Abinadi uses some familiar vocabulary in strikingly creative ways. But that's all part of why the text is so valuable.

For my part, I think Abinadi's explanation involves three basic steps. And each of these steps revolve around describing Christ's redemptive approach to "dwelling in the flesh" (see Mosiah 15:2).

In the argument's first step, Abinadi establishes that Christ, as God incarnate, is a combination of two divergent wills: the will of the flesh and the will of the spirit. Abinadi associates the will of the flesh with the Son and the will of the spirit with the Father. But, as Abinadi is using these terms, he's not talking about two different people or two different members of the Godhead. He's talking about the two kinds of wills that are conjoined in one life when a spirit "dwelleth in [the] flesh" (Mosiah 15:2). He's talking about what it's like to be alive "among the children of men" (Mosiah 15:1).

Now, as you've pointed out, in the second step of the argument, Abinadi makes clear that this flesh suffers. It sorrows. It grieves. It's silent. It's passive and filled with emotions and passions. The flesh—capable of suffering, available not only to act but to be acted upon—can be mocked and scourged and disowned. The flesh can die.

But, in itself, this capacity for suffering and passivity isn't a disaster. The flesh is not evil. It's not a curse. The flesh, after all, is precisely what Abinadi associates with the will of the Son, not with the devil. Christ is called "the Son, because of the flesh" (Mosiah 15:3). After all, we couldn't feel love if we didn't suffer passions. And we couldn't feel love if we couldn't be acted upon by those who love us.

How, though, do we redeem this flesh? How do we avoid being destroyed by these passions? How do we repurpose their strength and intensity in the service of life and creation?

For this to happen, the will of the Father and the will of the Son must become "one God" (Mosiah 15:4). This is the crux: "Thus the flesh becoming subject to the Spirit, or the Son to the Father, being one God, suffereth temptation, and yieldeth not to the temptation . . . . the flesh becoming subject even unto death, the will of the Son being swallowed up in the will of the Father. And thus God breaketh the bands of death" (Mosiah 15:5, 7–8).

Thus God breaketh the bands of death.

This is how Christ did it, just as you said: the will of the Son was "swallowed up in the will of the Father."

Or, to back up just a little bit, this is how Christ did it: the one God suffers temptation but yields not to temptation.

This is the description I keep coming back to: the one God, God incarnate, *suffers but doesn't yield.*

Without trying to defeat or escape or destroy the flesh—with all its joy and sorrows, passions and griefs—Christ willingly suffers . . . but doesn't yield. He feels these passions and sorrows with his whole soul, but they don't destroy him. Or, perhaps even better: Christ is able to feel them without being destroyed by them *because* he's willing to feel them with his whole soul. He's willing to feel both his own pain and ours. He's willing to sacrifice and submit. "He was bruised for our iniquities: the chastisement of our peace was upon him; and with his stripes we are healed" (Isaiah 53:5; Mosiah 14:5).

Christ is willing to suffer death without, at the same time, yielding to death. Christ is willing to die, but his willingness to die doesn't mean he's willing to let death win. Rather, Christ's willingness to die—to sacrifice his life for us—transfigures that death into a new life. Christ's atonement transfigures his death into a victory over death. Rather than avoiding death, Christ suffers death and, then, folds that death back into life.

And as his disciples, we must learn to join him on this same path. We must submit to the necessity of our flesh passing through that same "good night," even as we refuse to yield our spirits to that night. We must honor our anger and grief, even as we consecrate them again to God.

Adam

— CHAPTER 4 —

The Gospel of Alma

ALMA 7

After stepping down from the office of chief judge, Alma travels to the valley of Gideon to preach the word of God to the Church. He tells the people that the time is not far distant when the Redeemer will come to earth and live among his people. He prophesies that Mary will conceive by the power of the Holy Ghost and bring forth the Son of God. Christ will experience pains and afflictions of every kind, including death. He accepts death in order to unbind its chains for his people; he accepts suffering so that he knows how to succor them in their infirmities. Christ's bodily afflictions fill his bowels with mercy. Alma invites his listeners to be born again in baptism and to have faith in the Lamb of God.

"Cry unto this people, saying—Repent ye, and prepare the way of the Lord, and walk in his paths, which are straight; for behold, the kingdom of heaven is at hand, and the Son of God cometh upon the face of the earth." (Alma 7:9)

Adam,

Part of what makes this project different from our past scripture-related writings is the fact that we're comparing several passages. As you've mentioned, we decided to stick with the collaborative and close-reading strategies that have worked for us in the past, putting our heads together over small snippets of text and seeing what shows itself when we read slowly. But in this endeavor, unlike others, we're bringing a handful of different scripture passages together between the same two book covers. This adds another layer of discovery. Not only is each passage illuminated individually, but all of them together begin to manifest patterns, differences, echoes, and broader ideas about the Book of Mormon's unified witness of Christ.

When I'm studying several scripture passages together, after I have a basic handle on each one individually, I like to pick out a single element common to all—an image, a theme, or a phrase—and see how it works in each passage. In the gospel of Mary, I started thinking about the image of arms and hands. I was so struck by the specificity and tenderness in Nephi's vision of Mary "bearing a child in her arms" that I made it the central theme of my letter (1 Nephi 11:20). I was primed, then, to look for images of hands in the gospels of Benjamin and Abinadi. King Benjamin, that righteous king whose humility prepared his people to accept a heavenly King humble enough to become a man, reminded his listeners that

"I, myself, have labored with mine own hands that I might serve you" (Mosiah 2:14). Abinadi's hands make several appearances as well. He seems to have a habit of "stretch[ing] forth [his] hand" when he preaches (Mosiah 12:2; see also Mosiah 16:1). This makes it all the more striking when his body is bound and brought powerless before his accusers at his fiery death (Mosiah 17:5, 13). His hands stilled, he now preaches by giving his life. In this he, too, prefigures Christ.

Hands embracing and protecting, laboring and serving, actively teaching and passively bound: each image adds a different brushstroke to the Book of Mormon's portrait of Christ.

Hands are important in the gospel of Alma, too, both for what they symbolize and for what they do. Alma 7 records the sermon that Alma preaches to the Gideonites during the second stop of the preaching journey he undertakes soon after leaving the office of chief judge. He offers the people of Gideon a simple, poignant account of Christ's life that focuses on the grief and suffering the Savior willingly assumes for our sakes (Alma 7:11–13), and he invites them to follow Christ into the waters of baptism (Alma 7:14).

But before Alma ever arrives in the valley of Gideon, hands played a small but revealing role in Alma's backstory. His spiritual biography is one of the best-known stories in the Book of Mormon: his wickedness as a young man tears down the church of his father (Mosiah 27:8–10), he receives an angelic visitation (Mosiah 27:11), and he experiences a heart-cracking conversion to Christ (Alma 36:12–23). On previous readings, though, I'd never noticed that Mormon includes, in his description of Alma's coma-like period of spiritual rebirth, the detail that "he could not move his hands" alongside his inability to move his limbs, hear, or speak to the outside world (Mosiah 27:19; Alma 36:10–11). The loss of function in one's hands is deeply disabling—the very reason Abinadi was bound, of course—and the temporary paralysis of Alma's hands is the kind of vivid detail that makes a story come alive in my mind.

And maybe Alma's own memory of those stilled hands is part of what fuels him after a spiritual awakening restored the strength of his limbs. The man is a whirlwind of energy. Now that he can move his hands again, perhaps he decides that he will move them ceaselessly in the Lord's service. Mormon shows us scenes of Alma serving as high priest and as chief judge over his people (Mosiah 29:42); leading them into grim battle in the valley of Gideon (Alma 2)—the same place where he will later proclaim the gospel; and stepping down to dedicate himself to preaching (Alma 4:18–19). Then he's organizing and reorganizing congregations of believers (Alma 6:1), walking into a disaster and a miracle at Ammonihah (Alma 9–14), and dealing with Korihor (Alma 30). We catch glimpses of his hands during these scenes—wielding a sword against Amlici, for instance (Alma 2:31), and "laying on his hands" to ordain priests in Zarahemla (Alma 6:1). Alma is a man of powerful speech; there's no doubt about that. But he is also very much a man of urgent action.

All of these nuances of meaning shed light on a phrase that is uncommon in the Book of Mormon as a whole but characteristic of Alma's particular way of speaking: "the kingdom of heaven is at *hand*." Near the beginning of his sermon to the Gideonites, Alma reports that the Spirit has instructed him precisely on what he should say: "Repent ye, and prepare the way of the Lord, and walk in his paths, which are straight; for behold, *the kingdom of heaven is at hand*, and the Son of God cometh upon the face of the earth" (Alma 7:9; emphasis added). It's a phrase that appears at least five times in Alma's collected sermons, and related phrases appear even more frequently (see Alma 5:28, 50; 7:9; 9:25; 10:20).

This phrase brings to mind the words of John the Baptist, who similarly preached in the wilderness of Judea, "Repent ye: for the kingdom of heaven is at hand. . . . Prepare ye the way of the Lord, make his paths straight" (Matthew 3:2–3). For both prophets, the phrase "at hand" signifies the nearness of heaven, its looming approach in time and in space. The kingdom of heaven is coming, and it's close. There's work to be done and no time to be lost. The two men's shared language and shared urgency is appropriate; both were tasked with readying their people for the imminent coming of Christ.

All the whirlwind energy of Alma's hands laboring in the temple, in the courtroom, and especially in the mission field is channeled into his proclamation that Christ's coming is *at hand.* He wants his listeners to know—more than to know, to *feel* with urgency—that the kingdom of heaven is near. "There be many things to come," he tells them, but "there is one thing which is of more importance than they all—for behold, the time is not far distant that the Redeemer liveth and cometh among his people" (Alma 7:7).

For me, this is yet another brushstroke in the Book of Mormon's hand-drawn portrait of Christ.

Alma's urgency around the nearness of Christ's coming makes sense, given his personal history. In an instant, with no apparent warning, he was confronted in the road by an angel when he was least prepared, caught unaware in the throes of sin (see Mosiah 27; Alma 36). In a sense, the kingdom of heaven *did* come—for Alma, in that very moment—complete with apocalyptic thunder and earthquake, inexpressible light and joy, and a view of God on his heavenly throne (Alma 36:7, 20, 22). Alma understands that the timing of the kingdom of heaven is not just a question of cosmic history but of personal history. The kingdom of heaven is "at hand" because Jesus brings something of heaven with him wherever he goes. Where the King is, there is the kingdom. This is why Christ tells the Pharisees, as he sits with them, "The kingdom of God is in the midst of you" (Luke 17:21, ESV). Whenever we come near to Christ—whether through a willing opening of our hearts or through an unexpected encounter with an angel on the road—the kingdom of heaven is at hand, open for those who are worthy and willing to enter.

And if the Gideonites can be forewarned that the kingdom is very near, perhaps they can escape the "pains of a damned soul" that racked Alma for three days and changed him forever (Alma 36:16). I suspect that the process of preparing oneself for entry into the presence of God is never entirely comfortable; it always involves painful self-reckoning and searing sacrifice. But Alma has been warned and will not rest in the work of warning his neighbor (see Doctrine and Covenants 88:81).

If the expression "at hand" illuminates, at the opening of the sermon, the urgent nearness of the kingdom of heaven, I think the same image works in another way in the second half of Alma's gospel. After proclaiming the nearness of the kingdom, Alma proceeds to offer, as we've seen Benjamin and Abinadi do, a short account of Christ's life. He opens with Christ's birth to Mary, the virgin who conceived "by the power of the Holy Ghost" (Alma 7:10). But after describing the miraculous birth, Alma doesn't mention any other overtly miraculous or supernatural element in his gospel.

A good illustration is Alma's use of the phrase "go forth." As I mentioned in my first letter, this phrase appears often in our passages to describe Christ's ministry among his people. When Benjamin uses it, he says that Christ "shall go forth . . . working mighty miracles," including healing the sick and raising the dead (Mosiah 3:5). When Alma uses it, by contrast, something very different follows: Christ "shall go forth, suffering pains and afflictions and temptations of every kind" (Alma 7:11). In Alma's telling, Christ goes forth not to take away affliction, but to share in it. We don't see Christ's mighty miracles, miraculous healings, or cosmic signs of divinity. Instead, we see his sickness, death, infirmity, suffering—in short, we see the very things of which this life is made (see Alma 7:11–13).

Alma's gospel is made of the materials "at hand" in mortality. If the kingdom of heaven is at hand, as Alma proclaims, it's because Christ weaves heaven into earthly experience.

Alma is personally acquainted with supernatural manifestations—remember his encounter with the angel—and it's clear from his description of Mary's miraculous conception that Christ's divine identity is never in question. So why would Alma choose to deemphasize the otherworldly in his narrative of Christ's ministry? I think it's because he wants to teach us about the kind of redemption Christ offers us and about the deepest source of his power to save.

Christ's redemptive power, Alma shows, comes from a particular kind of knowledge: an embodied knowledge, a knowledge "according to the flesh." This phrase becomes a refrain in Alma's sermon. Christ willingly takes upon him the suffering and death of his people so that "his bowels may be filled with mercy, *according to the flesh*, that he may know *according to the flesh* how to succor his people according to their infirmities. Now the Spirit knoweth all things; nevertheless the Son of God suffereth *according to the flesh* that he might take upon him the sins of his people" (Alma 7:12–13; emphasis added). To save us, Christ needs to experience all that we experience. He needs the practical knowledge that can only come from a hands-on, full-body-contact life. This is the kind of knowledge that allows him to succor and save us, in our suffering and in our sin.

For me, this is the core insight of Alma's gospel. As the preexistent divine Word, Christ possessed a bird's-eye view of the entire plan of salvation. Infused with the Spirit, he knew "all things" (Alma 7:13). Yet he still needed to "know . . . *how* to succor his people" (Alma 7:12; emphasis added). He needed the practical knowledge, the know-how, that comes from living in a body with the world everywhere at hand, pressing in urgently with its welter of demands and dilemmas. He could only obtain this practical knowledge, it seems, by assuming a mortal body. Benjamin and Abinadi have already shown us vividly at what physical cost Christ won his redemptive know-how.

For me, there is no more beautiful illustration of Christ putting that practical know-how to work than his post-Resurrection ministry among the Nephites. Coming to a people undoubtedly traumatized by the terrifying darkness and upheavals that marked Christ's death (see 3 Nephi 8), the Savior demonstrates informed compassion in his gentle succor. In that most memorable scene of 3 Nephi 11, he invites each person present to probe the marks of the wounds that his body still bears (verse 14). He takes the time to do this, I think, both to confirm his divine identity and, I can't help but believe, to show a people who have been deeply wounded both individually and collectively that he truly mourns with them. He shows them that though they are wounded, they are nevertheless made in the image of God. Indeed, in their wounds they are *more* like him. I think Jesus's actions are the fruit of his mortal experience "according to the flesh." In some ways, this scene is the direct fulfillment of Alma's teaching that Christ took upon him a body, and with it our sufferings, so that he would "know . . . how to succor his people" (Alma 7:12).

A flood of implications flow from Alma's insight, it seems to me, but I'll conclude this letter with just two. One is about the nature of Christ's atonement. As Latter-day Saints, we are blessed with an especially rich theology of Christ's suffering in Gethsemane. Several passages of Restoration scripture—including, as we've seen, Benjamin's gospel—clarify for us the significance of Christ's ordeal in Gethsemane, where he agonized in blood and sweat and yet humbly submitted his will to his Father's (see Mosiah 3:7; Doctrine and Covenants 19:16). Alma's gospel, it seems, affirms the centrality of the suffering in Gethsemane by expanding its scope over the course of Christ's entire mortal life. But I see no evidence that Alma limits

Christ's vicarious suffering for our anguish to those pivotal and climactic hours in the garden. On the contrary, as I suggested earlier, the phrase "go forth" as it is used in Book of Mormon gospels typically suggests the entirety of Christ's ministry. In an expansive sense, Alma suggests, Christ's atonement determined not only the way he died but also the way he lived: in solidarity, in selflessness, in service.

And this brings me to my final point. If we are to follow Christ's injunction to "learn of me" (Doctrine and Covenants 19:23), it seems to me that we'll have to undertake the same kind of training in practical "know[ing] . . . how to succor" (Alma 7:12). As crucial as it is for me to understand the plan of salvation, to study the scriptures and the words of living prophets, and to seek for a perfect knowledge enriched by faith—none of that knowledge can be a substitute for practical knowledge of how to comfort, mourn with, and stand by my brothers and sisters. Learning how to change a bedpan, calm a crying baby, or speak to a bereaved widow is as essential as a Relief Society lesson or a Sunday discussion of President Nelson's most recent talk. Knowing how to build a wheelchair ramp, cook for a crowd, or listen to a troubled friend is as central to priesthood knowledge as reciting Doctrine and Covenants 6 from memory.

To learn of Christ is to engage our hands alongside our hearts and our minds.

Rosalynde

"Behold my beloved brethren, seeing that I have been permitted to come unto you, therefore I attempt to address you in my language; yea, by my own mouth, seeing that it is the first time that I have spoken unto you by the words of my mouth, I having been wholly confined to the judgment-seat." (Alma 7:1)

Rosalynde,

Alma the Younger is a preacher.

His calendar is full, and he keeps his hands busy. He rides the circuit from one church and city to the next. He starts in Zarahemla in Alma 5, then crosses the river eastward to Gideon in Alma 7, and then crosses the river again, westward, this time to Melek, Ammonihah, and eventually Sidom in the tragic and perilous chapters that follow.

More than this, he stops at all the places in between, apparently delivering some version of the same sermon again and again, doubtless shaping and sharpening it each time. Alma 5 certainly has the feel of a revival sermon that's been honed to pierce the hearts of everyone who hears it. And Mormon's own section heading seems to confirm as much when he describes Alma 5 as "the words which Alma, the High Priest according to the holy order of God, delivered" not only to Zarahemla but also "to the people in their cities and villages throughout the land."

Nephi writes in private of his (and Mary's) visions. Benjamin delivers a valedictory address at his son's coronation. Abinadi risks a messianic interpretation of Isaiah that costs him his life. But Alma—Alma not only belongs to the holy order of preachers, but he's also literally that order's high priest. He dedicates his life to it. Even before he's converted, he can't stop himself from preaching (see Mosiah 27:8–9). And even after he's appointed chief judge, he can't resist the call to trade all that power for a sturdy pair of sandals, an open road, and the word of God.

When he arrives in Gideon to deliver the sermon recorded in Alma 7, this is the first thing he tells them: "Behold my beloved brethren, seeing that I have been permitted to come unto you, therefore I attempt to address you in my language, by my own mouth, seeing that it is the first time that I have spoken unto you by the words of my mouth, I having been wholly confined to the judgment-seat, having had much business that I could not come unto you" (Alma 7:1).

When Alma preaches, he preaches with his own words. He uses his own language. Having "fasted and prayed many days that [he] might know these things of [himself]," he's not afraid to ground his preaching in his own firsthand experience of God (Alma 5:46). And now—finally—he's free to do so because he's no longer "confined to the judgment-seat" (Alma 7:1).

This choice of words doesn't feel accidental. Throughout these early chapters, Alma gives every indication that he really did experience the judgment seat as a kind of confinement, as a kind of detention or captivity, not because that work wasn't good or important but because that work wasn't preaching. Judging wasn't preaching. And for Alma, *not* preaching couldn't help but feel like a prison sentence, even if he was simultaneously the most "powerful" person in the land.

In this way, Alma reminds me of Jeremiah. Like Jeremiah, Alma might try to do some other kind of work for a time and, when it comes to God, "not make mention of him, nor speak any more in his name" (Jeremiah 20:9). But this can't last. Because when Alma dedicates himself to judging rather than preaching, then the word of

God, as Jeremiah says, "becomes like a fire locked up inside of me, burning in my heart and soul. I grow weary of trying to hold it in; I cannot contain it" (Jeremiah 20:9, NET).

Alma just can't do it. It's burning him up inside. He can't hold it in. He can't contain the word of God. He's got to preach.

(I have, in my own small way, felt this same fire shut up in my bones. In some other life, I can imagine myself a preacher, spending my days preparing Sunday sermons for one of Jane Austen's quiet parishes in the English countryside instead of shunting all that energy into teaching college freshmen Plato and Spinoza. I imagine that my parishioners would look on me with a dependable mix of bemusement, tolerance, and—occasionally, when I managed to speak in God's name—gratitude. All things considered, of course, I'm grateful to spend my days teaching Plato.)

But for Alma the problem isn't just about having enough time. It's not simply that being the chief judge keeps him so busy there's no room left for preaching. The dilemma goes deeper than this—and it goes deeper in a way that, I think, bears directly on Alma 7's description of Christ's own saving work.

For all the good that can be done from the judgment seat, Alma is keenly aware that the legal power he wields as a judge exists in *tension* with the power of God's word. In some vital way, his power as a judge undercuts his power as a preacher.

Alma knows that, if he steps down, the Nephites are still going to need "a wise man" to "enact laws" and "put them in force" (Alma 4:16). But Alma also knows that if he wants to preach, he must surrender that power. He must separate himself from the coercive force of their civil laws to fully avail himself of the noncoercive power of the word of God.

While laws are strong, Alma is convinced that the word of God is much, much stronger. He's convinced that only the word of God can heal his people. Only the word of God can "stir them up in remembrance of their duty" and pull down "all the pride and craftiness and all the contentions which were among [the] people" (Alma 4:19). And, as Alma sees it, there is no other way to "reclaim them save it [be] in bearing down in pure testimony against them" (Alma 4:19).

Again, this choice of words feels quite intentional. To reclaim his people, Alma's testimony must be "pure." But pure of what? His testimony must be purified of any coercive force. To preach, he must "come down" from his judgment seat so that he can "come unto" his people. To be with his people—to be one with them—his preaching must be purified of judging.

This same point gets repeated even more memorably in Alma 31. Alma wants to preach to the Zoramites because, as Mormon summarizes it, "the preaching of the word had a great tendency to lead the people to do that which was just—yea, it had had more powerful effect upon the minds of the people than the sword, or anything else . . .—therefore Alma thought it was expedient that they should try the virtue of the word of God" (Alma 31:5).

Here, the sentiment is the same. The word of God has a "more powerful effect upon the minds of the people than the sword, or anything else." But in order to "try the virtue"—that is, the power—of the word of God, Alma must first put down his sword. He must surrender his access to force. He can't preach with a sword in one hand and a gavel in the other. To preach, he needs his arms open and his hands free.

In just this way, Alma is a type of Christ, a weak reflection of the Messiah he announces in Alma 7:6–13.

In the first two verses of Alma 7, Alma describes himself four times as "coming unto" the people of Gideon or "coming now at this time." Then, in verses 6–9, he uses this same language four more times to announce the Messiah. Christ is twice described as "coming among" his people, he's described as he who "is to come," and he's described as "coming upon" the face of the earth.

Christ, like Alma, is coming. He's coming down from the heights of power and unto the people. And when he comes, he's coming to dwell among those people as one of them. He's coming into mortality to share in that mortality.

Alma never explicitly uses the word *condescension* in these verses. But his account of his own willingness to give up power and come down from the judgment seat has, I think, already set the scene for his presentation of the good news. Ultimately, I think what really sets Alma 7 apart from other gospel announcements are Alma's detailed descriptions of the *greater* power Christ now wields because he has come down to earth from heaven.

If you give up the judgment seat, separate yourself from coercive power, and come among the people, what are you enabled to do? What power are you granted? And why is this power so much stronger than the power of "the sword, or anything else" (Alma 31:5)?

As Alma describes it, it allows Christ to suffer with us.

"Coming unto us" allows Christ—as Alma repeats three times, with three critical variations—to "take upon" himself our burdens. It allows him to "take upon him the pains and the sicknesses of his people" (Alma 7:11). It allows him to "take upon him death, that he may loose the bands of death which bind his people" (Alma 7:12). And it allows him to "take upon him the sins of his people, that he might blot out their transgressions" (Alma 7:13).

And this work, as you emphasize, can't be done in the abstract. Because it's a question of practical knowledge, of hands-on know-how, it can't be done from a position of safety and power. It can't be done from the judgment seat. Even though "the Spirit knoweth all things; nevertheless the Son of God suffereth according to the flesh" so "that his bowels may be filled with mercy, according to the flesh, *that he may know according to the flesh* how to succor his people according to their infirmities" (Alma 7:13, 12; emphasis added).

These are remarkable verses, and there isn't anything else quite like them in scripture.

As Alma lays it out in these verses, we don't have any discussion of how Christ's suffering may appease a divine demand for punishment that balances the scales of justice. Rather, what we get is a cogent and detailed explanation of how his suffering in the flesh fits Christ to "take upon [himself]" not only death and sin but also "pains and afflictions and temptations of every kind," our sicknesses included (Alma 7:11). And by "taking" them, he delivers us from them. By suffering in the flesh, he can exercise "the power of his deliverance" according to the flesh (Alma 7:13).

Here the logic of atonement is straightforward: to save us where we are, Christ must come to where we are. To save us from our suffering, Christ must suffer with us and take that suffering upon himself. And, like Alma, he can't do either of these crucial things from the safety of a judgment seat.

"I came not to judge the world, but to save the world," Christ emphatically tells his disciples (John 12:47). And it's easy to imagine Alma greeting the people of Gideon the same way: I haven't come to judge, I've come to save. As powerful as the judgment seat seems, nothing is more powerful than God's promise that he's coming to live and suffer with us.

These verses in Alma 7 are almost enough to convince me that we should take Doctrine and Covenants 121:41's description of God's power at face value—"*no* power or influence can or ought to be maintained by virtue of the priesthood" (emphasis added)—and that, as a result, God's own power operates exclusively along a noncoercive axis.

Accustomed as we are to thinking that real power always comes from the coercive force of status and wealth and swords, it may be hard to believe that God's omnipotence truly works "*only* by persuasion, by long-suffering, by gentleness and meekness, and by love unfeigned; by kindness, and pure knowledge, which shall greatly enlarge the soul without hypocrisy, and without guile—reproving betimes with sharpness, when moved upon by the Holy Ghost; and then showing forth afterwards an increase of love toward him whom thou hast reproved, lest he esteem thee to be his enemy; that he may know that thy faithfulness is stronger than the cords of death" (Doctrine and Covenants 121:41–44; emphasis added). But this, nonetheless, is what these verses seem to say. True, love must sometimes reprove with sharpness—and we shouldn't doubt that the word of God is itself "quick, and powerful, and sharper than any twoedged sword, piercing even to the dividing asunder of soul and spirit"—but its power still comes from love, not force (Hebrews 4:12). And that love, God's love, carries the day only if its faithfulness proves stronger than the cords of death.

In this same spirit, one other unusual feature of Alma 7 stuck with me as I studied it. In this chapter, in the context of Alma's need to separate judging from preaching, Alma twice uses a word that neither he nor anyone else uses again in scripture.

Alma twice describes his people's sinful state of pride and rebellion as a "dilemma." In verse three, he expresses his hope that he will not find the people of Gideon "in the awful dilemma that our brethren were in at Zarahemla." And in verse eighteen, he expresses his relief that the people of Gideon "were not in the state of dilemma like [their] brethren."

To experience a "dilemma" is, literally, to find oneself caught between two (*di*) paths or propositions (*lemmas*). It's a situation that requires a hard choice between difficult alternatives.

This, it seems to me, is a remarkable—and remarkably clinical, precise, and nonjudgmental—description of what it feels like to be a sinner.

As a sinner, I don't often *feel* like an enemy to God. I don't often feel like a rebel, full of pride and bent on my own destruction. I don't doubt that as a sinner, I am, in some sense, an enemy and a rebel. But being a sinner rarely feels this way. In my experience, what sin feels like, instead, is a dilemma. Sin feels like being stuck. It feels like being trapped by bad choices—and then making more bad choices. It feels like being caught between a rock and a hard place.

Maybe this is what Alma starts to understand about sinners once he surrenders his position of power to be with his people. Maybe this is what he, like Christ, comes to know—not just in theory but "according to the flesh"—about the nature of a sinner's sinning as they suffer, grow old, and die.

When Alma stops judging and starts preaching, maybe this is what he sees: that sin, rather than being a war, is a dilemma. And once he feels this in his bones, perhaps he's prepared to speak in God's name and help liberate the people from it.

Adam

— CHAPTER 5 —

The Gospel of Abish

ALMA 19

Abish is a servant in the court of the Lamanite king Lamoni, where the Nephite missionary Ammon has recently arrived to preach the gospel. After learning of Christ, Lamoni falls into a state of joyful insensibility in which he sees a vision of the radiant Redeemer, who will be born to a mortal mother and will redeem humanity. Lamoni's subsequent testimony of Christ's incarnation causes many in the court to fall unconscious in the same way. The servant Abish, who was herself converted to Christ by a "vision of her father" many years ago, seeks to share the good news with the neighboring community, and a crowd gathers at the palace. Turmoil ensues. Abish, in hopes of restoring order, takes the Lamanite queen by the hand and raises her back to consciousness. The queen arises and blesses the name of Jesus. Many onlookers believe, and the first Lamanite church is established.

"And it came to pass that she went and took the queen by the hand, that perhaps she might raise her from the ground; and as soon as she touched her hand she arose and stood upon her feet, and cried with a loud voice, saying: O blessed Jesus, who has saved me from an awful hell!" (Alma 19:29)

Adam,

The gospel of Abish is a birth story. It's the story of God doing a new thing in the world.

I arrived in Castelo Branco, Portugal, in May 1996, a new missionary in a new vineyard. Castelo Branco sits in the lap of a white castle that guards the Mediterranean plain unrolling from highlands to the east. The shadow of the castle falls over the Jardim do Paço Episcopal, the Garden of the Bishop's Palace, a quadrangle of graceful boxwood curves lined with processions of stone kings memorializing a history of strife and dominion. My companion and I would walk there sometimes, chatting up anybody who would speak to us.

It wasn't until 1974, following the overthrow of Portugal's authoritarian regime, that the first Latter-day Saint missionaries arrived in Portugal. And Castelo Branco, near the Spanish border, didn't receive badge-wearing young people until the early 1990s. When I was there, members of the Church would reminisce about the earliest gatherings of their branch—simple meetings of song and prayer and testimony offered outdoors among the statuary of the Jardim. God was doing a new thing there. Beneath the stone rulers and the bloody past over which they presided, he was unveiling a new kingdom ruled by the Prince of Peace.

God was doing that same work, birthing a new kingdom, in the palace of the Lamanite king where Abish served. Before that time, formal missionary efforts among the Lamanites had failed, maybe because previous Nephite missionaries came among Lamanite communities with too much of the old stone kings and too little of the Prince of Peace in their countenances (see Enos 1:20). But God worked a secret wonder with Abish and her father, and when Ammon comes into the land as a servant, everything changes. Mormon sums up the marvelous events in Lamoni's court like this: "Thus the Lord did begin to pour out his Spirit upon [the Lamanites]; and we see that his arm is extended to all people who will repent and believe on his name" (Alma 19:36).

All gospels are birth stories. The gospel of Abish is the birth story of Lamanite Christianity.

As we planned this chapter together, we decided to name it after Abish, even though that seemed counterintuitive to me at first. After all, Ammon is the missionary who preaches Christianity to the Lamanite court, and the king and queen are the converts who speak their testimonies. We know that Abish has also been converted to Christ and that her actions are decisive in the events that unfold, but in what sense can we call this chapter Abish's gospel? As you and I discussed it, we realized that her testimony-in-action is the crucial catalyst for the harvest of souls that occurs in the Lamanite palace. And it's possible that, in editing the records, Mormon may have drawn on something like Abish's personal account of those events, perhaps including her own secret conversion to Christ. How else could Mormon have known of Abish's actions and motivations, given that every other eyewitness was temporarily unconscious (see Alma 19:16–19)? On the whole, it feels right to give Abish's name to this powerful Book of Mormon story.

But if Alma 19 is Abish's gospel, it's quite unlike the others we've considered so far. At first, its gospel content seems so slight that it hardly qualifies for the genre. Alma 19's formal proclamation of Christ's life consists entirely of Lamoni's statement to the queen upon his (first) awakening, "Blessed be the name of God, and blessed art thou. For as sure as thou livest, behold, I have seen my Redeemer; and he shall come forth, and be born of a woman, and he shall redeem all mankind who believe on his name" (Alma 19:12–13).

For all their brevity, these few lines pack a powerful theological punch. Remember that Lamanite religion in the time of Lamoni seems to have centered around belief in the Great Spirit (Alma 18:5). We know little about this deity, but it seems safe to say that Lamanites understood God to be intangible and incorporeal. The doctrine of incarnation, of God-become-flesh, would have been unknown. And, given Ammon's explanation of heaven in the previous chapter (Alma 18:28–32), it seems safe to infer that the doctrine of divine condescension, God's crossing from heaven to earth, was likewise unknown among the Lamanites.

So in Lamoni's elegantly brief statement that Christ "shall come forth [from heaven], and be born of a woman," he introduces two central tenets of the gospel of Jesus Christ: the condescension of God and the incarnation of Christ. Three, in fact, for if Christ is born of a woman, it is implied that he will die as a man. Mortal birth comes bundled with eventual death, as surely for the Son of God as for you and me. Lamoni introduces Mary, though he does not say her name, as the key to these doctrines of condescension, incarnation, and atonement. Positioned between heaven and earth, Mary is the gateway through which Christ passes in his journey of transformation from "Father" to "Son."

That's all we get from Lamoni, rich as those few lines are. If this is a gospel, an account of the good news of Christ's birth, life, and death, it's a pretty slim one.

But sometimes gospels are shown, not told.

In the events of Alma 19, many of the elements of Christ's life as it was told and retold by the Nephite prophets do actually show up—but they show up divided, recast, and distributed among the Lamanite characters as they interact in this remarkable story. For instance, I've noticed as we've worked through these texts that the Book of Mormon gospels, like the New Testament gospels, almost always show Christ healing the afflicted (see 1 Nephi 11:31; Mosiah 3:5; Alma 7:12). And indeed, in Alma 19 we see a similar healing, though it occurs not in an account of Christ's life, but in the interaction between two people. The Lamanite queen attests the revival of her husband with tender attention and exemplary faith, echoing the Christ's healing of the centurion's son as recounted in Matthew 8. The extraordinary faith of the centurion and the queen places these two scriptural stories together as an instructive pair. Of the Roman centurion's confidence that his son would be raised, Jesus says, "I have not found so great faith, no, not in Israel" (Matthew 8:10). Similarly, Ammon says of the queen's confidence that her husband will rise again: "I say unto thee, woman, there has not been such great faith among all the people of the Nephites" (Alma 19:10). When I read of the queen's faith and the king's revival, I see Christ's words and actions with the centurion reenacted in the context of the Lamanite court.

The parallels between prophesied events in Christ's life and events in the Lamanite court continue throughout Alma 19. For example, Benjamin's gospel shows us Jesus Christ "raising the dead" (Mosiah 3:5). In the gospel of Abish we also see the dead—or apparently dead—raised into new life. Abish raises the queen in a sequence of events that typologically calls to mind Christ's raising of Lazarus (Alma 19:29; John 11).[9]

In their gospels, Benjamin and Abinadi speak of the "mighty miracles" manifest in Christ's ministry (Mosiah 3:5; 15:6); in the gospel of Abish we see the queen expressing the ecstasy of her conversion in miraculous gifts of language (Alma 19:30).

Book of Mormon gospels emphasize Christ's compassionate anguish for the wickedness of his people, often expressed as "the bowels of mercy" (Mosiah 15:9; see also Alma 7:12); here we see Abish "exceedingly sorrowful, even unto tears" (Alma 19:28) when she witnesses the violent contention in the court where there should have been wonder and Spirit.

Nephi sees followers of Christ fall down in worship (1 Nephi 11:24), and, well, you get the idea. Suffice it to say, there's plenty of falling in the Lamanite palace.

The gospel of Abish is a gospel in action. The events of Christ's life are enacted in the founding story of the Lamanite church: in the queen's faith and miraculous gifts, in the king's rising, in Abish's raising of the queen, and in her extraordinary compassion and service. This has always been the proper relationship between the gospel and the Church: the Church reenacts and shares the truths originally embodied in Christ's life. The life of Christ was always meant to overflow the borders of his own body, always meant to be divided and distributed everywhere two or three gather in his name. In our tiny branch in Castelo Branco, we enacted Christ's baptism on Saturday afternoons, our new friends dying and rising with Christ in white jumpsuits and a portable tub in the storefront where we met. We enacted his prayer, teaching our friends to bow their heads and address God with the words "Nosso Pai Celestial." We enacted his last meal, swallowing his body and blood every Sunday morning after the sacrament hymn. Almost every day, events of Christ's life leapt off the page and into the shadow of that white castle overlooking a Mediterranean plain. Gospels of Jesus Christ leap off the page in the rituals and practices that mark every life of discipleship.

If the gospel of Abish, the birth story of the Lamanite church, stages the events of Christ's life in a new way, it does so with a new spirit as well. The Book of Mormon, as we've seen, emphasizes the depth of Christ's suffering and vulnerability even at the height of his divine power. The Son of God is "a man of sorrows, and acquainted with grief," and this somber reality gives a matching mood to many of the gospels we've explored. Alma 19 introduces a new tone: joy. Four times in this story, we're told that the many characters who sink to the ground do so because they are overcome with joy (Alma 19:6, 13, 14, 30). Mormon, the editor of the story, sees the joy and light imparted by the gospel of Christ as the direct cause of the serial spiritual swoonings that punctuate this story: after Lamoni proclaims his brief gospel, "his heart was swollen within him, and he sunk again with joy" (Alma 19:13). The gospel of Abish stages a memorable performance of "the glad tidings of great joy" that Benjamin received from the angel (Mosiah 3:3).

What is joy? Why is it expressed in the death-like spiritual slumber that spreads through the Lamanite court? It's true that, historically speaking, religious communities have expressed spiritual emotion in unique behaviors transmitted through culture, and joyful swooning in the Spirit seems to work that way in the Lamanite conversions. But I don't think that's the whole story. I think joy shows up in this story to convey something specific about life and death in a world governed by a God who took upon him both. I think the gospel of Abish brings some theological rigor to the idea of joy. In particular, I think it tells us that joy comes from reseeing our life's movement toward death as the image of Christ himself.

I've suggested that Lamoni's proclamation of Christ's life sketches, in minimalist fashion, the doctrines of the condescension, the incarnation, and the atonement of Christ—and that these teachings were extraordinary for a people who had never thought of God as living and dying in human terms. Conversion to Christ demands a commitment to follow him in life and in death, a commitment we celebrate and seal with baptism. In baptism, we follow Christ into his death and burial and follow him out of that watery grave into new life. Mormon tells us that the newly converted Lamanites were soon baptized (Alma 19:35). I wonder if their many sinkings and risings in the Spirit at the house of the king can be seen as a kind of practice for their future baptisms, as spontaneous, symbolic rehearsals of their commitment to follow Christ into death and new life. They experience this "practice" death and resurrection with joy. Overcome by new life in Christ, Lamoni's conversion "infused such joy into his soul, the cloud of darkness having been dispelled . . . that the light of everlasting life was lit up in his soul" (Alma 19:6).

Joy felt from the inside doesn't always look like joy from the outside. The middle of Abish's three-act story resembles the end of *Hamlet*: a dismal display of the dead strewn among agitated onlookers, and only one witness who can "speak to the yet unknowing world / how these things came about" (5.2.379–80). In the Lamanite palace, however, the scene mingles the dead with the only-apparently dead. And as if surveying a field of wheat and tares, it's not always clear which is which. Who is really dead? Who is really alive in Christ? It takes a certain kind of seer to detect the difference. Ammon sees. The queen sees. Abish sees. These seers perceive by the light of a Son whom others don't yet know. They are already living in the new kingdom.

I think this is what joy means in the gospel of Abish: not merely general happiness and gratitude, but the experience of seeing and pursuing the radically new reality of the kingdom of God, a reality in which death is defeated not by forestalling it with force, but by practicing it in the image of Christ. We practice death not only in baptism or spiritual swoonings, of course; we practice Christlike death and resurrection in every act of godly self-sacrifice. As Jesus taught, "whosoever shall seek to save his life shall lose it; and whosoever shall lose his life shall preserve it" (Luke 17:33). It's important that Jesus taught that truth when answering a question about the coming of the kingdom of God (Luke 17:20). Sometimes we think about the kingdom of God as a distinct millennial era in the future, and sometimes we think about it as the Church established here on earth. Jesus taught us a third way to think of it: the kingdom of God is the new perspective that comes from seeing and practicing death and resurrection in the image of Christ, which paradoxically opens onto a life of joy. As Mormon describes Lamoni's experience of this new perspective, "this light had infused such joy into his soul, the cloud of darkness having been dispelled . . . that the light of everlasting life was lit up in his soul" (Alma 19:6). This hasn't been an easy lesson for me to learn, as I've raged at death these last few months. The gospel of Abish has come as a gift and a daunting challenge at the same time.

In the Lord's Prayer, Christ invites us to share in—to enter into—his own prayerful reality of the Father's "kingdom come" (Matthew 6:10). The kingdom of God isn't always visible from the outside: once inside, we go about our lives among the same people and places that defined our previous lives. The Lamanite palace is still the Lamanite palace when Lamoni awakes. But a new King sits on its throne. Adam, in your book *An Early Resurrection,* you've written that we enter this new reality when we rise in Christ from the waters of baptism, enacting his resurrection.[10] The gospel of Abish stages resurrection after resurrection, and portals to the kingdom open in every joyful breath.

I think we can add one last detail to this gospel's theological portrait of joy. Yes, joy is what it feels like to witness the birth of a new kingdom, to see the only-apparently dead pulsing with life and light and spirit. Joy is perceiving and pursuing the reality of the kingdom of God. But even more specifically, joy is what it feels like to live under the new King, a servant-king who defeated his enemies, sin and death, by embracing them. Joy, in other words, is what happens when, following Christ and his disciples, like Abish and Ammon, we exercise power with disarming love rather than overpowering force. Joy is what is produced when the first makes itself last and the last is thereby made first.

We see this joy all over the place in the gospel of Abish. Inherited ladders of domination are turned on their sides and repurposed as bridges. We see it in the prologue story of Ammon the servant-missionary, who levels his people's sense of ethnic superiority and approaches the Lamanite community as a servant, not a master (Alma 17:25). We see it in the two women, Abish and the queen, who upend inherited patterns of gender domination by inhabiting as women the healing role of Christ (Alma 19:11, 29). Most of all, perhaps, we see it between the two women, who invert expected patterns of social domination as Abish becomes the spiritual and narrative center of the story. The servant and her queen reverse positions in anticipation of the servant-Savior whose kingdom they now inherit (Alma 19:29).

The effect of these reversals is not to rebuild equal-but-opposite ladders of domination, on which the new-first now grind the faces of the new-last. The point instead is to repurpose these ladders as bridges of connection, across which we can grasp one another by the hand. Abish understands this: "And it came to pass that she went and took the queen by the hand, that perhaps she might raise her from the ground; and as soon as she touched her hand she arose and stood upon her feet, and cried with a loud voice, saying: O blessed Jesus" (Alma 19:29). In the joining of hands, mistress and servant join their joy in Christ, their witness of Christ, and their rising in Christ.

The gospel of Abish is a nativity. It's the birth of a new kingdom in the garden of the old kings.

Rosalynde

"And it came to pass that they did call on the name of the Lord, in their might, even until they had all fallen to the earth, save it were one of the Lamanitish women, whose name was Abish, she having been converted unto the Lord for many years, on account of a remarkable vision of her father." (Alma 19:16)

Rosalynde,

Something happened to Abish.

It happened many years before the events related in Alma 19. It happened behind the scenes, offstage, outside the frame of the Book of Mormon's own way of telling its story. And when it happened, it changed her—acutely, substantially, indelibly. It reordered some core part of her. It touched some fundament buried deep below the surface of her mind.

And, as a result, she was "converted unto the Lord" (Alma 19:16).

This is what I want to understand. This is what I want to see: this unseen moment when she was changed. I want to understand what changed her and I want to understand exactly *how* it changed her.

I want to know what it means to be "converted."

This, after all, is what the previous four gospels have been promising, isn't it? This is what Mary, Nephi, Benjamin, Abinadi, and Alma have all seen and all promised: that God is coming to save me. That God is coming to change me. That God is coming to "convert" me into something new.

But what does this mean? What does it mean to be converted? What new thing will I be?

This is a hard question. And it may be especially hard to answer for Abish because she barely flickers into view, for just a split second, at the far edge of the Book of Mormon's field of vision.

What happens to Abish happens deep in enemy territory, outside the bounds of Nephite society. In a book centered on Nephite men, it happens to a "Lamanitish" woman (Alma 19:16). And in a book dominated by kings and armies, it happens to a "woman servant" (Alma 19:28).

But still, there she is: a flash of lightning that changes *everything* that follows in the Book of Mormon. Abish's story *is* a nativity story.

Incredibly, Abish is "converted unto the Lord" without any missionaries, without any church, without any scriptures, without any rituals or ordinances, simply "on account of a remarkable vision of her father" (Alma 19:16). And then, "having been converted unto the Lord, and never having made it known" (Alma 19:17), she just continues on like that, changed but silent, redeemed but invisible.

And this, essentially, appears to be all we know about what happened to her. We know the bare minimum. We know the least we could know without knowing nothing.

But what if, in this case, the bare minimum is actually an advantage?

What if the lack of complicating variables actually makes it easier to isolate the few that matter most? Because, while we know only the bare minimum about what happened to Abish, it's also true that she, in turn, appears to have *experienced*—without missionaries, churches, scriptures, or ordinances—something like the bare minimum needed for conversion.

As you put it, Abish may be an excellent case study in gospel minimalism.

Clearly, Abish's conversion left her hungry for the fullness of the gospel, and when she sees it, she recognizes it. But in the absence of that fullness, what was the minimum? What sort of change was so powerful and so essential that, even without that fullness, she counted as "converted unto the Lord"? In starvation conditions like these, what are the bare essentials?

I suspect that Abish may be a good example of what the Catholic theologian Karl Rahner called an "anonymous Christian." Or, similarly, what the Lutheran theologian Dietrich Bonhoeffer called an "unconscious Christian." An anonymous Christian is someone who, like Abish, has been "converted unto the Lord" without knowing how to name it. Something decisive has happened to her and she's faithful to it, but she lacks the Church's ready-made tools—its shared scriptures and formative rituals—for sealing that change, sharing it, and making it fully conscious. She remains silent about what happened to her, at least in part, because she doesn't know how to explain it or talk about it. She keeps it to herself because she doesn't know how to share it.

What if, rather than first being converted to the intermediary of a religion, Abish was simply—directly, immediately—converted "unto the Lord"?

To be sure, this spare way of reading Alma 19 is only one possibility. But, to me, this angle seems worth pursuing. If we treat Abish as an unconscious Christian—as a case study in gospel minimalism—something essential may come into focus.

Take, for example, the one detail we *are* explicitly given about the vision that catalyzed her conversion. Abish, Mormon reports, was "converted unto the Lord for many years, on account of a remarkable vision *of her father*" (Alma 19:16; emphasis added). This is a good place to start, but as many readers have noted, it's not clear what this curt description means. Is Mormon reporting that Abish's father had a vision and then Abish was converted by what her father saw? Or is Mormon reporting that Abish had a vision of her father that then led to her conversion? Did Abish see something through her father's borrowed eyes? Or did Abish see her father with her own eyes?

Both readings are viable. But as a case study in gospel minimalism, I'm inclined toward the latter. I'm inclined to see the vision as her own. I'm inclined to see her as an agent in her own story. And, if this is the case, then I'm also inclined to think it would only be natural for her unconscious conversion to be catalyzed by a vision—specifically—of her father.

We might take this as the first rough data point to be extracted from our case study: that the essence of conversion is, in some way, intertwined with family.

If conversion changes who we are in a fundamental way, then conversion must also change something fundamental about our relationships with the people we've depended on most, with the people whose influence has shaped our hearts and minds at the earliest and deepest levels. God couldn't convert one without also converting the other.

Or, to frame this same point more broadly: conversion must be intertwined with family because conversion requires that we be reconciled with the necessity of our deep and ongoing *dependence*—both our dependence on one another, especially and originally our parents, and ultimately our dependence on God.

To be converted, we must be reconciled to the fact that we didn't make ourselves; that we depend on others for who we are, what we want, and what we have; and that true joy is always shared. To be converted we must be reconciled to the fact that we cannot be made perfect without them, nor they without us (see Doctrine and Covenants 128:15).

If this is true, then our first data point may simply be this: that conversion hinges on a dawning consciousness of our dependence.

For any additional data points, though, we'll need more information. We'll need some way to look deeper into Abish's mind. And to do this, we'll need a little creativity—or, as you've said, a little "informed imagination"—to help us close that gap.

For my part, I think Alma 19 may contain two more hidden doors that offer glimpses into Abish's mind and the substance of her unconscious conversion.

To this end, it's useful to note that the whole of Alma 19 is about people falling over unconscious—and, what's more, that the whole chapter also turns on exactly what happens to these people *while* they're unconscious.

And, as Joseph Spencer once pointed out in some long-lost blog posts, Abish finds herself smack in the eye of this storm of unconscious kings, queens, and servants. As he outlined the chapter, the story of Alma 19 is structured to emphasize this.

Ammon teaches King Lamoni. The king falls unconscious. And once the king is unconscious: enter the queen.

The queen worries over the king. The king wakes up, tells the queen about his conversion, and then falls unconscious again—followed, like dominoes, by the queen, Ammon, and all the attendant servants. And once the queen is unconscious: enter Abish.

As the lone servant still standing, Abish gathers a multitude and wakes the queen. But once the queen is conscious again: exit Abish.

The queen then wakes the king. But once the king is conscious again: exit the queen.

The king preaches, multitudes are converted, and nothing is ever the same again. The end.

As this brisk outline highlights, the chapter's narrative structure operates like a set of revolving doors. When one player exits, another enters. When one returns, the other disappears. The queen enters the story once the king is unconscious, and she immediately exits the story when he's fully conscious again. And, too, Abish enters the story only once the queen is unconscious and then immediately exits the story once the queen is conscious again.

In sum, the queen pops into the story like a manifestation of the king's unconscious, vanishing again once he's conscious. And Abish, in turn, pops into the story like a manifestation of the queen's own unconscious, vanishing again once the queen wakes.

We don't need this narrative structure to bear a lot of weight—though I do love its suggestive symmetry. But it does link Abish to the mind of the queen and the queen to the mind of the king. And, in this way, it hints at the possibility of an additional door into Abish's own mind: verse six of Alma 19.

In Alma 19:6, Mormon gives a truly remarkable description of what happens in Lamoni's mind while the king is unconscious. Mormon's description goes like this:

> Now . . . [Ammon] knew that king Lamoni was under the power of God; he knew that the dark veil of unbelief was being cast away from his mind, and the light which did light up his mind, which was the light of the glory of God, which was a marvelous light of his goodness—yea, this light had infused such joy into his soul, the cloud of darkness having been dispelled, and that the light of everlasting life was lit up in his soul, yea, he knew that this had overcome his natural frame, and he was carried away in God.

The description itself is amazing. But before considering what it says, it's worth a moment to appreciate the sheer fact that this description exists.

The description we get in Alma 19:6 is three layers deep. We get Mormon's narration of what Ammon knows about what's happening in the unconscious mind of King Lamoni. We get Mormon looking inside of Ammon's mind looking inside of Lamoni's mind.

Now, I don't think Mormon was implying that Ammon literally looked into Lamoni's unconscious mind. Rather, Mormon seems to be reporting that Ammon had a strong spiritual intuition about what *must* be happening in Lamoni's mind.

How would Ammon know what must be happening in Lamoni's mind?

Ammon would know, I think, because he'd already witnessed Lamoni "cry unto the Lord, saying: O Lord, have mercy" (Alma 18:41). He'd witnessed Lamoni pray for conversion. And then he watched as Lamoni "fell unto the earth, as if he were dead" (Alma 18:42).

So, Ammon doesn't need to guess or have supernatural access to Lamoni's mind to know what's happening. Ammon knows from the inside out—from his own experience of being knocked flat by an angel in Mosiah 27—exactly what happens in the dark sub-basement of someone's mind when they undergo conversion: the lights turn on.

We might take this as the second data point to be extracted from our case study. Conversion "lights up the mind." And by showing us what, as sinners, we've been hiding from ourselves, that light changes something fundamental about how the mind works.

I suspect we could spend a long time taking Alma 19:6 apart, bolt by bolt. But for now, there are just three key moments I want to foreground as Lamoni is "converted unto the Lord." Looking into Lamoni's mind, Ammon knew from his own experience: (1) that Lamoni must be "under the power of God"; (2) that this power was like a "light which did light up his mind," dispelling a "dark veil of unbelief"; and (3) that this light also "infused such joy into his soul" that "he was carried away in God."

How do these pieces fit together? Perhaps they fit as follows.

Lamoni finds himself "under" the power of God. His dependence on God's power is revealed to him. The light of this truth dispels the trap of "unbelief" in which he's been caught: the trap of thinking that he doesn't need God or depend on God. And once this "cloud of darkness" is dispelled and his dependence on God is revealed, Lamoni's approach to happiness is fundamentally rewired. Rather than trying to find some contingent happiness independent of God, he finds himself infused with a joy that follows immediately from embracing his dependence on God. In short, Lamoni trusts God—he believes what he's seen, he faithfully affirms his dependence on God, he lets God prevail—and allows himself to be carried away in God.

If Ammon is right, if something like *this* change is essential to every experience of conversion, then perhaps we might confidently say the same of Abish. If Ammon can look into Lamoni's unconscious mind, then we might use this same side door to glimpse Abish's conversion.

Abish had a vision of her father. And if this vision of her father resulted in her "conversion unto the Lord," then she must have experienced her deep dependence on God's power and, then, a fundamental rewiring of how she pursued happiness.

Which brings me to the second hidden door, the final testimony borne by "*all* the servants of Lamoni"—perhaps including Abish; why not?—at the end of Alma 19. "And it came to pass that when Ammon arose he also administered unto them, and also did all the servants of Lamoni; and they did all declare unto the people the selfsame thing—that their hearts had been changed; that they had no more desire to do evil" (Alma 19:33).

Take this as the third and final data point we might extract from this case study. Here, all the king's servants declare "the selfsame thing": conversion changes the heart. Conversion changes what we desire and how we desire it. Conversion fundamentally rewires—at the deepest, unconscious levels—what we want and how we pursue happiness.

A changed heart—a heart or mind that has been "converted unto the Lord"—is a heart that has no more desire to do evil. A changed heart now depends on God's will, not its own, for happiness.

This, I think, is what happened to Abish.

This is what happened behind the scenes, offstage, outside the frame of the Book of Mormon's story. This is the essential change that qualifies Abish as a Christian—even if, before Ammon arrived, she'd never heard that word. Even if, for a time, she bore Christ's name anonymously, unconsciously.

Something like this specific change is the bare minimum needed for conversion and redemption. And without it—without this transformative firsthand experience of my dependence on God—all the "religion" in the world can't save me.

My own circumstances could hardly be more different from those of Abish. From the start, I've had all the advantages she didn't. I was born a Christian, sealed in the covenant, destined for the priesthood, and named in the records of the Church before I could even talk or crawl. My whole life has been full of meetings and scriptures and rituals. My heart and mind were shaped at the deepest and earliest levels by my parents, their devotion to the Church, and their love of God. Without any doubt, this has been a great blessing.

Over the years, though, I've found myself walking the same path as Abish—but backwards. I've worked and studied and fasted and prayed to get *back* to that spare, anonymous place where she started, where she found herself converted unto the Lord, an unconscious Christian, before she could even name what had happened.

Abish started out with God and eventually found the Church.

I started out with the Church and have spent my life searching for God.

And, ironically, the closer I've come to the bare essentials of her anonymous Christianity—the closer I've come to a naked experience of the divine minimum—the more rooted I find myself in the Church and its scriptures and its rituals.

Adam

— CHAPTER 6 —

The Gospel of Samuel

HELAMAN 14

The Lamanite prophet Samuel is called to preach the word of God in the Nephite city of Zarahemla, which has fallen into wickedness. Denied entrance, Samuel mounts the city wall and warns the Nephites that disaster awaits: four hundred years in the future, he prophesies, the Nephite nation will be utterly destroyed. In the meantime, their material possessions will be cursed and their civilization will disintegrate into violence and greed. Their only hope is Jesus Christ. An angel has visited Samuel with the glad tidings that Christ will soon come into the world, will suffer much, and will be slain for his people. The sign of his birth, which will occur in five years, will be two consecutive days with no dark night between them, together with other heavenly manifestations. The sign of his death will be three consecutive days of profound darkness, together with great and terrible terrestrial upheavals. Samuel teaches that Christ's death redeems humankind by bringing about the Resurrection, which returns each person to the presence of God.

"Behold, I, Samuel, a Lamanite, do speak the words of the Lord which he doth put into my heart; and behold he hath put it into my heart to say unto this people that the sword of justice hangeth over this people." (Helaman 13:5)

Adam,

Can I make a confession? I've carried a grudge in my heart for a long time, a grudge against the book of Helaman. One Christmastime years ago, I read the book of Helaman as I prepared a Church lesson. I guess I came to the text wanting to find Jesus, preferably in sweet baby form, with cinnamon-scented candles and warm fuzzies to match the season. Instead, all I could see was wrangling, retribution, and curses. By the time I got to the sermon of Samuel, the Lamanite prophet who foretold a day of days and a night of nights, my heart was closed. I wasn't willing to look for Christ there. I still believed in it as scripture, but for a long time I read the book of Helaman without real intent to find Christ.

Since then, my love for the Book of Mormon and my testimony of its truth have grown sweeter each year. I attribute that growth to the time I've spent reading it slowly. I've been lucky enough to do some of that slow reading in seminars with you, surrounded by our colleagues' sharp minds and good souls. But most of that reading has been pretty ordinary—preparing seminary lessons, reading with my kids, keeping up with the Church curriculum. Over time, my heart has softened, too, as life has served me the hard-crust course it saves for the middle-aged.

So I owe an apology to the book of Helaman, and to the Lamanite prophet at its climax, for closing my heart to its message and misreading its gospel. To this end, I've written a story, a kind of parable, as a gift of contrition. Nobody would ever mistake me for a gifted tale-teller, but this is my effort to do justice, after my heart closed years ago, to what I've since come to recognize as the profound and compassionate gospel of Jesus Christ preached in this text. Here's my story.

> There was a woman who had two sons. The day came for her departure to the high pastures where the sheep summered. She called her sons to her. "While I am away," she said, "you must place a lamp in the window every evening. I will look for the lamplight in the valley, and when it shines steadily I will raise my lantern. Look to the highlands in the north and east, and you will see the yellow light burn. Thus I will know that you abide at home, and you will know when I drive the sheep to new pasture." She showed them how to fill the lamp, trim the wick, and adjust the flame. Then she departed for the high country.
>
> Every evening as darkness fell, the sons did as she asked. The younger raised the window shade, and the elder checked the fuel and lit the lampwick. Together they placed the burning globe on the sill and looked into the darkening distance. Every evening they saw their mother's golden light answer on the high horizon, shedding its faint gleam below the stars.
>
> The season of ripening melons and thunderheads arrived in the valley. One afternoon, the elder son said to his brother, "Tonight we will not light the lamp in the window. We are no longer babes who cry at the dark. I am going to the village and will not return until the hour is past. Mother has likely driven the sheep far away and will not look for the lamplight tonight." So they did not light the lamp that night, nor raise the shade to look for the answering gleam.

They did not raise the shade the next night, either, nor the next, and the lamp glass grew dim on a low table.

After a long time, the vines withered around the fat melons and darkness came early in the evening. One night the younger son's eye fell on the cold lamp, and he felt ashamed. He went to the window and lifted the shade. No golden flame answered his gaze on the high horizon. But he did see the cold gleam of a beast's eye. "Brother!" he cried. "We are lost! Wolves circle the valley! Mother and the sheep have perished, and we cannot fly to the mountains for safety!" The brothers scrambled beneath the floorboards, where they trampled bushels of apples and scattered green cheeses in their terror.

When cracks of light appeared above their heads, the boys crept upstairs and peered through the window. Far away they saw their mother returning across the lowland. They ran to the door. "Mother! Do not come here! Wolves stalk the valley and will scatter the sheep. Their eyes burned from the hills in the night!"

Their mother entered and replied, "You foolish, slothful boys! You failed to light the lamp. You were ashamed to look for my answer and suppressed the witness of your own eyes. What you saw in the hills was not the eye of a beast but the gleam of my lantern. It burned for you last night as it has every night from the high pasture. In your fear, you have spoiled the provisions I laid up against the season. This winter will be lean indeed, my children."

That's my parable, shared here, with some embarrassment, as a peace offering to the book of Helaman. I'll come back to it later to explain how I intended it to echo Samuel's gospel. First I'll dive into the prophet's own words.

It's my hunch that Samuel has only one message, one essential theme at the core of his extended sermon: "The sword of justice hangeth over this people" (Helaman 13:5). That's it. That's the message. God's justice waits in heaven, soon to make itself known on earth. But Samuel takes the long way in driving this message home.

In part, this is because the Lamanite prophet preaches to a flip-flopped Nephite society, one in which every structuring story has been inverted. In the gospel of Abish, we saw the beginning of the sweeping cultural transformation through which the Lamanites replaced the Nephites as the keepers of Christianity (Helaman 6:1). They now observe the law of Moses and teach the doctrine of Christ among themselves with unwearied diligence (Alma 25:15). They believe the scriptures and the prophecies and have been led by faith and repentance to a change of heart (Alma 25:16). They are firm, steadfast, and free, having buried their weapons of war and turned away from sin (Alma 24:19).

The Nephites, by contrast, have slid ever further into frenzied cycles of political violence and wealth seeking. They reject the words of the prophets and deny the prophecies of Christ. They bury themselves in status-fueled feuds and all manner of sin, just as vainly as they bury their wealth in the ground (see Helaman 13:20). Their church is in disarray, and their missionary efforts permanently stalled. Now, indeed, the Lamanites must send missionaries to the Nephites, an ironic inversion of the scene in Lamoni's court (Helaman 6:4). The only reason Zarahemla has not already been destroyed, Samuel warns, is that a righteous minority endures within its walls. "But behold, if it were not for the righteous who are in this great city," Samuel says in the voice of God, "behold, I would cause that fire should come down out of heaven and destroy it" (Helaman 13:13).

The sword of justice is set to drop, and nothing can save the Nephites except repentance and faith in Jesus Christ. Samuel's formal gospel, his narrative account of Christ's incarnation and redemptive death, is brief but covers the essentials: Jesus Christ "shall come into the world, and shall suffer many things and shall be slain for his people" (Helaman 13:6). Mortal birth, a life of sorrows in solidarity with humankind, and a death offered for his friends: it hits the notes that we've come to expect in the Book of Mormon's several witnesses of the life of Christ.

It's possible that Samuel—or Mormon—encodes a scriptural hyperlink to King Benjamin's fuller account, which was also delivered from a perch high above the same city more than a hundred years previously. Samuel quotes twenty-one words of Benjamin's gospel, naming the source of Nephites' salvation in "Jesus Christ, the Son of God, the Father of heaven and of earth, the Creator of all things from the beginning" (Helaman 14:12; quoting Mosiah 3:8). When Samuel speaks these names, his audience may be prompted to remember Benjamin's description of the Lord Omnipotent who comes down from heaven to suffer every kind of bodily anguish for his children. One scholar—my father-in-law, in fact—has wondered whether these names of Christ were incorporated into Nephite worship services and transmitted through missionary work to the Lamanites.[11] This would explain how they roll so easily and precisely from Samuel's tongue. When the Nephites hear from the mouth of a Lamanite these sacred archaic words for Christ, long neglected in the disarray of the Nephite church, I can imagine that the syllables pierce to the core.

A sword hangs above their heads. Jesus Christ is their hope of salvation.

This is Samuel's one message. But under its banner, he braids two different prophecies. First, he warns of the extinction of the Nephites that will occur in four hundred years (Helaman 13:9). The Nephites' incorrigible wickedness finally ripens to their own destruction, as the hearts of their brethren—Samuel's own people, the Lamanites—turn against the Nephites in fraternal violence

(Helaman 13:8). It's hard to fathom how devastating this message must have been to any open-hearted Nephites who listened to Samuel's words—and to Samuel himself, who would have realized that this prophecy of the Nephites' physical destruction might also entail the spiritual destruction of his own people, who would "dwindle in unbelief" and return to the patterns of violence that they had so courageously overcome in their recent conversion (Helaman 15:11).

And then, of course, Samuel famously utters a second prophecy, this one much nearer in the future. In just five years, he promises, Jesus Christ, whose life he briefly summarized earlier, will come to earth to redeem believers. His coming will be heralded by a brilliant day of days: the night before the Son of God is born, there will be no darkness among the Nephites (Helaman 14:2–5).

In some ways, these two prophecies seem like opposites. The coming of Christ into the world is the ultimate good news of the gospel: even the sun and stars celebrate God's loving-kindness. The Light of the World is revealed in the order of creation. On the other hand, the prospect of the Nephites' ultimate judgment is shocking, and Samuel's stomach-turning description of their future extinction appalls in its violence and wrath (Helaman 15:1–2).

But as Samuel's sermon continues, the two prophecies seem to join hands. Samuel teaches that there's a counterpart to the signs of Christ's birth. The sign of his death, the extended night of nights during which all the lights of the sky hide their faces, will be followed by the destruction of Nephite cities, including Zarahemla and her people, in cataclysms of natural upheaval. As Samuel foretells these disasters, the violence and suffering he describes become indistinguishable from the suffering of the Nephites at their final destruction. Indeed, he seems to purposely layer the two prophecies into one another, mingling their imagery and transitioning seamlessly from one scene to the next. For example, at the transition between Helaman 14 and 15—noting, of course, that this chapter break exists only in modern Book of Mormon editions and not in the original version—Samuel moves directly from the destruction of unbelievers at Christ's death (Helaman 14:29) to warnings of the Nephites' final desolation (Helaman 15:1). At first it's difficult to tell which timeframe Samuel is addressing; only as Helaman 15 proceeds do we come to understand that he has returned to the four-hundred-years-in-the-future prophecy (Helaman 15:17).

Why does Samuel nest and mingle the two prophecies—of Christ's coming and of the Nephites' judgment—in this way? I think it's because he sees both prophecies, in their apparent opposition, as twin expressions of his one theme: "The sword of justice hangeth over this people" (Helaman 13:5). I think he wants us to see the sword and the Savior as one and the same. I think he wants us to see Jesus Christ as that instrument of God's justice hanging over the world, about to descend from heaven to earth to do his Father's work. The gospel and the prophecies are united in a single message. God's mercy and God's judgment are united in the person of his Son. Justice and mercy come together in his single, ever-loving action in the world: the gift of his Only Begotten.

You taught me to see things this way, Adam, in your book *Original Grace.* There, you showed me that God's response, to good and to evil alike, is always love. God returns good for our goodness, and he also returns good for our wickedness. Rather than giving us what we deserve, you argue, God gives us what we *need* to learn, grow, and heal. And so, you write, "if justice is the art of giving whatever good is needed—and not, instead, the business of giving only what's deserved—then justice and grace are two names for the same thing."[12] God's sword of justice, in other words, is identical to his instrument of mercy. If this is true, then the "sword" of justice that Samuel evokes is not a symbol of God's punishment of the wicked, but a symbol of his love's power to do right by all of his children. The sword and the Savior are one and the same.

It's taken me some time to get used to this way of seeing things. In particular, I've had to keep in mind what it doesn't mean: it doesn't mean that there are no consequences for sin. Samuel's prophecy of the fate of the Nephites in the Book of Mormon drives that truth home unmistakably. And on the other hand, it also doesn't mean that everything we suffer in life is given to us by God because we somehow "need" it. Much of our suffering is simply baked into the shape of existence, and some is brought on by our own fear and reactivity, as we also see in the story of the Nephites' destruction. We don't need to believe that suffering, our own or others', is God's "tough love" strategy. I've seen how harmful that misconception can be to a person's trust in God.

But if Samuel's prophecies of the sword and Savior are one and the same, what should we make of the Nephites' misery, described so vividly in these chapters? Isn't this God's sword of punishment exacting the penalty for their centuries of wickedness? Another scripture comes to the rescue here—the first chapter of the book of Romans. In this passage, the Apostle Paul makes a profound observation about the way we experience God in the world. When we are open and reconciled to God in faith, he teaches, we experience his love everywhere in the world around us, in the cycles of creation as well as in the events of Christ's redemption. "Ever since the creation of the world," Paul explains, "God's eternal power and divine nature, invisible though they are, have been seen and understood through the things God has made" (Romans 1:20, NRSV). But when we separate ourselves from God through sin, that same love begins to feel oppressive and threatening to our autonomy. We start to see God's steady love as judgment of our own unloving behavior. And instead of experiencing God all around us, we evict God from our lives and tell ourselves that he is condemning us from a faraway heaven. As Paul puts it, "The wrath of God is revealed from heaven against all ungodliness and injustice of those who by their injustice suppress the truth" (Romans 1:18, NRSV). In this way, God's unchanging love all around us begins to feel like punishing wrath threatening us from above. God's promise of a Savior begins to feel like a sword hanging over our head.

In our tragic, self-generated shame and fear of God's wrath, in our frenzied attempts to escape it, we create a hell of destruction and misery. That's not on God; that's on us. This, I think, is Samuel's point in a horrifying passage late in his sermon in which he describes the fate of nursing and pregnant mothers as the Nephites seek to escape their final destruction. In their frenzied flight, Samuel says, nursing and pregnant women will be trodden under the feet of the swift, trampled and left to perish in their gore (Helaman 15:2). In the context of Samuel's proclamation of the coming birth of Jesus Christ, it's hard to imagine a more shocking image than the slaughter of innocent mothers and infants. Perhaps Samuel included this image, despite its violence, to make it clear that the Nephites' destruction is, at least in this moment, tragically self-generated by their own fear and reactivity.

Maybe you can understand why my heart closed to Samuel's gospel all those years ago. The slaughter of innocents is not an easy image to forgive. But as I now understand it, that passage is vital to Samuel's purpose: to show that the sword and the Savior are one and the same, that God's justice is love—without denying the consequences of sin. It would be no gift to the Nephites to deny the reality of sin and of the misery that follows. But Samuel's essential message, as I see it, is one of hope and compassion: God's love does not fail. The Savior waits in heaven. He returns good for good and good for evil.

And maybe you see now what I was trying to say in my parable of the mother's lantern. The lantern shines steadily every night from the hills. When her sons turn toward the light, they see its golden glow as the warm confirmation of their mother's love. But when they turn away, they forget what that love looks like. Their shame and fear convince them that the lantern is the threatening glare of a beast. And in their frenzied effort to hide, they destroy their own refuge. It will be a long and lean winter; there's no escaping that reality. But since I'm the author of the story, I can tell you that they get through it with their mother. The lantern's light never goes out.

Rosalynde

"And behold this is not all, there shall be many signs and wonders in heaven. And it shall come to pass that ye shall all be amazed, and wonder, insomuch that ye shall fall to the earth. And it shall come to pass that whosoever shall believe on the Son of God, the same shall have everlasting life." (Helaman 14:6–8)

Rosalynde,

I think there's some truth to the old saying that, to a man with a hammer, everything looks like a nail.

So, too, it's easy for philosophers to think that all life's problems can be solved with a little more thinking. It's easy for people who read books for a living to conclude that what we really need is to read more books.

To hammers, everything looks like a nail. To thinkers, everything looks like a riddle. To readers, everything looks like a book.

I try to guard against this temptation. I try to stay skeptical about the importance of words and ideas. I try to keep an eyebrow raised when I hear myself talking about how crucial it is—especially in religion—to know things and read things and understand things. Many of the most important things in religion are decisively about the heart, not the head.

But, still, sometimes you need a hammer. Sometimes that nail is a nail.

And sometimes, as Samuel tells the Nephites, our salvation really does turn on being able to read and understand the "signs" God is giving us.

I take this to be the point, in many ways, of your own surgically sharp parable. That lantern shining from the hills is a sign. But will the boys look for the sign? And if they do look for it, will they read it as a sign of love or a threat? And if they do read it as a sign of their mother's love, will they offer the right sign in return?

I'll grant that sometimes, given distance or absence, signs are the best we can do. But as your parable shows, signs are often fraught and fragile things. For me, this same persistent emphasis on the importance of signs—despite their obvious weakness—is what stands out as most unique and unusual in the gospel according to Samuel. To this point, we haven't seen anything quite like Samuel's marriage of sign and gospel.

As you note, in Helaman 14, Samuel tells the Nephites of cosmic signs—the two days of light and the three days of darkness—against the backdrop of Helaman 13's oracle of destruction. "The sword of justice hangeth over this people," Samuel warns, "and four hundred years pass not away save the sword of justice falleth upon this people" (Helaman 13:5). This oracle is then developed in grim detail through a series of *wo*'s. And the whole prophetic cycle is topped off with an elaborate curse that takes up Helaman 13's final twenty-two verses. The Nephites will come to think, Samuel prophesies, that their "land is cursed" because, they'll say, "all things are become slippery, and we cannot hold them" (Helaman 13:36; compare Helaman 13:17–39).

But as you've prompted us to ask—what's the nature of this curse? Who, in truth, has cursed whom? And what does the curse mean?

To start, Samuel presents the curse as the word of the Lord. He says, "hearken unto the words which the Lord saith; for behold, he saith that ye are cursed because of your riches, and also are your riches cursed because ye have set your hearts upon them" (Helaman 13:21).

But as he wraps up the cursing in Helaman 13:38, Samuel also presents the curse not as God's special intervention but as an inevitable consequence of the people having "sought all the days of your lives for that which ye could not obtain; . . . ye have sought for happiness in doing iniquity."

Did God curse the Nephite treasures, making them unusually slippery? Or are earthly treasures just always slippery, disappointing, and untrustworthy objects of love?

Here, as with any sign, meaning is itself slippery. The curse itself requires interpretation.

Additionally, when Samuel repeats in Helaman 15 the "wo" initially pronounced in Helaman 13, he appends a surprising explanation: "The people of Nephi hath [God] loved, and also hath he chastened them; yea, in the days of their iniquities hath he chastened them because he loveth them" (Helaman 15:3).

The wo and the curse, Samuel claims, are somehow good for the people. They are actually signs of God's love, not of his anger or hatred.

But this tendency to misread God's signs is, of course, part of what it means to be a sinner: as sinners, we get stuck in sin because we can't correctly interpret the real meaning of our own actions—or God's.

Choosing evil over good, we naturally, inevitably get evil. And then when God, out of love, still turns this evil into an occasion for good—i.e., into an occasion for "chastening," for reformation and repentance and reconciliation—we blame God for punishing us with the evil we insisted on choosing in the first place.

The problem isn't that God insists on punishing us with evil. (God doesn't do evil, even in response to our evil.) The problem is that we're foolish enough to think we can choose evil without, then, the natural consequence of getting the evil we've chosen. The problem is that we're foolish enough to think wickedness could ever be happiness (see Alma 41:10), while the truth all along, as Samuel says, was that "whosoever doeth iniquity, *doeth it unto himself*" (Helaman 14:30; emphasis added).

As sinners, we suffer from this inability to read the signs and see what's real. We continually misinterpret evil as good and good as evil. And, so, we continually get more evil. And then we blame God (rather than our own actions) for the evil we suffer—thereby refusing accountability for these consequences and outsourcing that burden of responsibility to God in the form of a divinely mandated "punishment."

If we suffer, we think, it must be God's doing, not our own. If God hadn't punished us with evil, we tell ourselves, we could have gotten away with evil. As if evil weren't already evil!

What, though, could be more predictable than sinners refusing responsibility for their own actions? Or, as you put it, what could be more predictable than sinners misreading God's love as wrath?

And this, I think, is a useful backdrop for the cosmic signs that organize Samuel's account of the gospel in Helaman 14.

In Helaman 14, Samuel offers two sets of signs: one set marking Christ's birth and one set marking Christ's death—mute monoliths made of weather, light, and sky that memorialize, like a pair of boundary stones, the span of God's mortal life.

The set of signs marking Christ's birth centers on the arrival of "one day and a night and a day" when "there shall be no darkness" (Helaman 14:4, 3). The sun will go down, Samuel emphasizes, but it will look "as if it were one day and there were no night" (Helaman 14:4). Then in addition to these forty unbroken hours of light, Samuel also predicts there will be "a new star" and "many signs and wonders in heaven" (Helaman 14:5, 6).

The parallel set of signs marking Christ's death centers, then, on a black three-day span during which "the sun shall be darkened and refuse to give his light" (Helaman 14:20). The moon and stars will also go dark, and this darkness will be filled with the clamor of storms and earthquakes and death.

These signs are all very dramatic, and appropriately so. But Samuel doesn't get caught up in the drama of the signs themselves. Instead, each time Samuel introduces a sign, he quickly moves to add to that sign a prophetic description of the "intent" that animates it.

With respect to the signs of Christ's birth, Samuel explains that he wants the Nephites to "know of the signs of [Christ's] coming, to the intent that ye might believe on his name" (Helaman 14:12).

And with respect to the signs of Christ's death, Samuel (quoting an angel) offers a whole string of interlocking intentions as justification. The signs were given to the Nephites, he says, "to the intent that they might believe that these signs and these wonders should come to pass upon all the face of this land, to the intent that there should be no cause for unbelief among the children of men—and this to the intent that whosoever will believe might be saved" (Helaman 14:28–29). Here again we get intentions added to our signs—but now we get those intentions wrapped inside other intentions, wrapped inside other intentions, wrapped inside of signs. But in both cases, all of these signs are clearly and unequivocally anchored to God's single-minded intention to save us.

What should we make of Samuel's cosmic signs? And, perhaps more urgently, what should we make, in general, of signs in relation to the work of salvation?

To start, I'm not sure how to think about the importance of cosmic signs like these. I'm not sure how to think about what role they could—or even should—play in my conviction that Jesus is the Christ. And I especially don't know what to do with these particular cosmic signs. The post-Einstein cosmology that informs my understanding of the universe could hardly be more different from the assumed cosmology of Samuel's first-century audience.

But, more to the point, I can't help thinking that signs are, in general, a slippery, oblique, and strange way to help save people. If our salvation is at stake, why work through signs at all, let alone ambiguous signs in the sky animated by divine intentions nested three layers deep? Why not take a more direct approach?

As best I can tell, Jesus himself seems mixed on the value of signs.

John tells us that Jesus performed "signs" to reveal his glory. He changed water into wine "as the first of his miraculous signs [*semeion*], in Cana of Galilee" and "in this way he revealed his glory, and his disciples believed in him" (John 2:11, NET).

Jesus also told his disciples to watch for signs of his return, telling them that before "they see the Son of man coming in a cloud with power and great glory," there would be "signs in the sun, and in the moon, and in the stars" (Luke 21:27, 25).

And Jesus told his disciples that "signs shall follow them that believe; In my name shall they cast out devils; they shall speak with new tongues; they shall take up serpents; and if they drink any deadly thing, it shall not hurt them; they shall lay hands on the sick, and they shall recover" (Mark 16:17–18).

But Jesus also warned his disciples against the seductive dangers inherent in signs, "for false Christs and false prophets shall rise, and shall shew signs and wonders, to seduce, if it were possible, even the elect" (Mark 13:22).

And most emphatically, Jesus sharply criticized those who, "except [they] see signs and wonders . . . will not believe." He told those who asked him for "a sign from heaven" that only "a wicked and adulterous generation seeketh after a sign; and there shall no sign be given unto it, but the sign of the prophet Jonas" (John 4:48; Matthew 16:1, 4).

Clearly, different people have faith in Christ for different reasons at different times in their lives. But I suspect that, for me, even dramatic cosmic signs like Samuel's would do little to move the needle of my faith in Christ one way or the other. And, to be honest, I'm not sure if this is a good or bad thing.

What to do, then?

While I don't have any final answers, I do have a theory. And before we leave Samuel, I'd like to sketch this idea about when signs have redemptive value.

My theory, roughly, is that signs with redemptive value always point to God *in* the world, not to God *outside* the world.

Or, again: my theory is that signs have redemptive value when they indicate how God's presence is already operative and available in this world, rather than when, in God's presumed absence, they appear to function as signs of his transcendent reality beyond this world.

Where the first kind of sign nurtures faith in Christ's active and ongoing presence in this world—and, thus, is redemptive—the second kind undercuts it by implying God's absence.

Samuel's cosmic signs are good examples, I think, of the first kind, the redemptive kind, of signs. Both sets of cosmic signs are meant to herald Christ's arrival in this world. They mark Christ's arrival in the flesh and bear witness to the reality of his suffering and death.

Instead of being placeholders for an absent God, they're designed to function as a wake-up call. Their "intent" is to shock us awake so that we can see firsthand, with our own eyes, that God is here—now, in person, in this world, in the flesh—and he's ready to heal us, forgive us, suffer with us, and die for us.

These cosmic signs were designed, Samuel says, with the intent "that ye shall all be amazed, and wonder, insomuch that ye shall fall to the earth" (Helaman 14:7). And then, rocked from our self-absorbed stupor, we might finally see what's already obvious and "believe on the Son of God" (Helaman 14:8).

But for Samuel, God's presence in our world isn't limited to the span of Christ's mortal life. It appears that, for Samuel, God is always present, always close at hand. God is always with us. God is "not far from every one of us: for in him we live, and move, and have our being" (Acts 17:27–28). Indeed, the whole earth is already filled with the glory of the Lord (see Isaiah 6:3). It's just a question of whether, through faith and repentance, we will open our eyes and acknowledge the reality of God's ongoing presence.

In this spirit, Samuel announces that "the resurrection of Christ redeemeth mankind, yea, even *all mankind*, and bringeth them back into the presence of the Lord" (Helaman 14:17; emphasis added). And further, Samuel claims, it's only this restoration to God's presence that "bringeth to pass the condition of repentance" (Helaman 14:18).

Here, surprisingly, being in the presence of God is described as "the condition" for repentance. And if repentance is possible now, in this life, then it seems that we must—in some crucial way—already be in God's presence.

Clearly, in one sense, repentance restores us to the presence of God. But in another sense, God's rescuing presence is the condition that makes repentance possible in the first place. If God hadn't already come to rescue us—if the resurrection of Christ hadn't, from all eternity, already redeemed "all mankind"—then the conditions for repentance wouldn't exist. Repentance would be impossible.

In this way, repentance isn't just about getting *back* into the presence of God. Repentance is about our willingness to confess that God is already present. Repentance is about our willingness to *live*—hour by hour, day by day, even in our weakness—in the presence of God. But if we aren't willing to stay in God's presence, then all will be lost again. In the end, the unrepentant will be "hewn down and cast into the fire; and there cometh upon them *again* a spiritual death, yea, a second death, for they are cut off *again*" (Helaman 14:18; emphasis added).

Which brings me full circle to my theory of signs: that the point of a sign with redemptive power is to call me back to this work of repentance, to wake me up to God's presence—here and now—in this world, and to aid my efforts to continue in this presence forever.

That, at least, is my reading.

But if this approach captures something important about the purpose of divine signs, I wonder if we might retell your parable one more time, but with an additional twist.

Could we imagine a version of the parable where the signs of the mother's love point to her presence rather than her absence? A version where, if we had eyes to see and ears to hear, we could bring into sharp focus the reality of God's active and ongoing presence in this world?

If our eyes were open and single, what could stop them from being full of light?

Adam

— CHAPTER 7 —

The Gospel of the Brother of Jared

ETHER 3

The brother of Jared ascends Mount Shelem, carrying sixteen small stones in his hands. He asks the Lord to touch each stone so that they will shine in the darkness of the Jaredite barges. The Lord does as he asks, and the brother of Jared falls to the earth with fearful astonishment at the sight of the Lord's finger. The Lord teaches that he will take upon him a body of flesh and blood at his birth. He then reveals to the man the complete image of his preexistent spirit body, bringing the brother of Jared fully into the divine presence. The Lord introduces himself as Jesus Christ, the Father and Son, and shows the brother of Jared that all humanity is made in Christ's own divine image. He promises that all who believe in his name will become his sons and daughters and will have life eternally. He shows the brother of Jared a vision of all things and instructs him to write and seal the things he has seen.

"And the veil was taken from off the eyes of the brother of Jared, and he saw the finger of the Lord; and it was as the finger of a man, like unto flesh and blood; and the brother of Jared fell down before the Lord, for he was struck with fear." (Ether 3:6)

Adam,

When I was growing up, my mother was a prodigious note writer. Her handwriting is minuscule, developed in college to save paper, and I learned young how to decipher those straight-ruled lines of tiny ballpoint script. She would write me notes when she was proud of me, when she was worried about me, or when she had something hard to talk about. For a couple of years my younger brother was in and out of the hospital unpredictably, and I'd often come home from school to find a note from her on the counter: "In the hospital with Jacob tonight. Dinner is in the fridge and Daddy will be home by bedtime. Love, Mama."

These notes told me, at least in part, that she was away from home. If she were home, she wouldn't have to leave a note, right? She'd just be there.

Don't signs necessarily imply absence? Isn't their whole function to stand in for a person or a meaning that can't be fully present? Doesn't God give us signs precisely because he's not here?

You asked me to think about a new version of my parable in the last chapter, a version in which God's signs point to his presence, not his absence, in the world. This is a different way of thinking about signs—signs do not stand in place of God's presence but rather are a part of God's way of being present with us.

And it makes beautiful sense. After all, my mother often wrote me notes when she was present at home. The note wasn't a substitute in her absence but a way of showing that she was there for me. And when she did have to be at the hospital, her notes told me that she was present in spirit, that she loved me and was thinking about me: she was *with* me, even if she was away from home. Her notes were an expression and completion of her love—a tiny-lettered, blue-inked slip of a sign for the inexhaustible ocean of love from which she has drawn to bless and nurture me from the day I was born until this very moment.

But, as we saw in Samuel's gospel, signs can be misinterpreted. It wasn't easy to read my mom's handwriting, and some words I couldn't decode. If God gives us signs in order to share himself, then I guess that means that even when we are close to God, we must communicate across the space between us. Sometimes when we interpret wrongly, we'll have to repent, learn more, try again, and forgive. Maybe being willing to risk this is part of what Samuel means by the "condition of repentance." As you wrote, "repentance is about our willingness to *stay* in the presence of God"—our willingness to do the work that union requires.

It strikes me that we see precisely this process—of interpreting, mistaking, learning, and repenting—play out in Ether 3, the story of the brother of Jared's mountaintop encounter with Christ. At the climax of the narrative, the brother of Jared finds himself being drawn "within the veil," as Moroni puts it, that holds Christ's presence in the world (Ether 3:19). At the very moment when Christ begins to show himself to the brother of Jared, the man misinterprets what he sees. When he perceives Christ's finger, he falls to the ground in terror, explaining that he "saw the finger of the Lord, and . . . feared lest he should smite me" (Ether 3:8). He makes the same interpretive mistake the Nephites do in Samuel's prophecy: the brother of Jared assumes God's presence is inaccessible to the world, concealed and buffered by a thick protective cloud, and so misinterprets Christ's dawning body as an omen of dread. He reads God's gesture, his reaching toward humanity, as a threat of punishment rather than an invitation to abide together.

Unlike the Nephites, the brother of Jared does not try to escape his initial misinterpretation; he does not flee the punishment he believes is coming. Instead, he steadies himself, looks and listens a bit longer, and rises to stand when Christ calls him. He trusts God. And because he leans into his trust rather than his fear, he enters into Christ's full presence. He's taught to read the true meaning of Christ's body: not an instrument of punishment, but the manifestation of God's love and the fulfillment of his promise to be with us. Condescension. Immanuel. "For God sent not his Son into the world to condemn the world; but that the world through him might be saved" (John 3:17).

I've never connected these two passages—Samuel's horrific prophecy of the Nephites' fatal panic when attempting to flee, and the brother of Jared's first fear at the finger of the Lord (Helaman 15:2; Ether 3:6). But now I'm convinced that the same error of interpretation and the same emotional logic are at play. When we banish God from our world and look for him only with a telescope, expecting that he is far away, he appears threatening and angry. When we instead look for him close by, when we use a magnifying glass instead of a telescope, we see that his hand is extended in blessing, not in violence.

There's always something new to see in Ether 3.

I've already told you how I quarreled with Samuel the Lamanite and then repented and opened my heart to his message. In contrast, the brother of Jared has been a faithful companion over the past few years. In 2019, I spent half the year buried in the record of Ether almost every day as I studied its theology for the first book I ever wrote. And each year since then has brought another project that turns me back to the third chapter of Ether. All roads lead to Mount Shelem, it seems. Reading upon reading of those twenty-eight verses has rewarded me with fresh discovery. The story of the brother of Jared's mountaintop encounter with God, its symbolism and its primal themes, speak to my soul in a way that, in my whole life, I may never fully fathom.

There's a moment I especially love in the brother of Jared's conversation with Christ. The veil has just been taken from the man's eyes, and he sees the finger of Christ reach for the stones, in every appearance like the finger of a man (Ether 3:6). In astonishment, the brother of Jared confesses to the Lord that he has seen his finger, a shocking occurrence because he "knew not that the Lord had flesh and blood" (Ether 3:8). With gentle correction, the Lord teaches that "[he] *shall* take upon [him] flesh and blood" in the future (Ether 3:9; emphasis added). He then asks the simple question that jolts me every time I read it: "Sawest thou more than this?" (Ether 3:9)

I think Christ is asking not only what the brother of Jared has perceived with his eyes, but also what he has learned or "seen" in understanding—what he has seen about the Savior's incarnation, his condescension, his mission in the flesh. I hear Christ asking, in part, "Do you understand more about me?" It's a question that seems directed to me, the reader, as much as to the brother of Jared. After studying this passage, bottomless in its interpretive depth and theological richness, do I, Rosalynde, sister of Jacob, see more of the Savior?

The brother of Jared, with equal parts honesty and spectacular courage, answers, "Nay; Lord, show thyself unto me" (Ether 3:10).

This question is easier for me to answer. When I've come to Ether 3 with sincerity of heart and real intent, more often than not, I can answer, "Yes, I've seen more."

Though the brother of Jared is never formally called a "seer" in the book of Ether, there's no doubt that he's a gifted see-er. I've long thought that the brother of Jared and the prophet Enoch make a fascinating study in contrasts. As Enoch's story unfolds in Moses 6, Enoch hears the voice of the Lord instructing him to "anoint thine eyes with clay, and wash them, and thou shalt see" (Moses 6:35). When Enoch completes this earthy ritual, resonant with scriptural echoes, "he beheld the spirits that God had created; and he beheld also things which were not visible to the natural eye; and from thenceforth came the saying abroad in the land: A seer hath the Lord raised up unto his people" (Moses 6:36). Enoch has become a seer because he is able to see across time something that is hidden for others—namely, the spirits of humankind created at the origin of the cosmos.

The brother of Jared's experience complements Enoch's in compelling ways. When the veil is removed from the brother of Jared's vision, he too is able to see across time something that is hidden for others. But where Enoch sees spirits, the brother of Jared sees a body, the body of Christ. And where Enoch sees spirits created in the past, the brother of Jared sees the Lord as he will appear to his people in the future. Enoch is a seer of creation; the brother of Jared is a see-er of incarnation.

Not only does the brother of Jared see the spirit body of Christ, and "see" the truth of the Savior's embodiment in the flesh, but he also sees something about his own body. "Seest thou that ye are created after mine own image?" Christ asks. "Yea, even all men were created in the beginning after mine own image" (Ether 3:15). What we see of Christ's spirit body through the eyes of the brother of Jared sheds light on our own embodiment. As we've discussed, Benjamin, Alma, and others often use their own embodied experience as a lens to understand Christ. Here the lens is flipped: Christ's (spirit) embodiment teaches us to understand our own bodies, what they are and what they are for. I'll have more to say about that in a moment.

You and I agreed that we should include this story in our exploration of the Book of Mormon's accounts of Christ's life even though we recognized that it differs in some significant ways from the other gospels we've read together in these pages. The biggest difference, of course, is that the brother of Jared personally sees and experiences the Christ-who-will-come-in-flesh, rather than learning about his life from an angel, a prophet, a missionary, or a scriptural text. Consequently, the brother of Jared doesn't give us a narrative of Christ's mortal life, beginning with birth and ending with death or resurrection, in the way that our other passages do. Instead, he narrates his own encounter with the premortal Christ, giving a snapshot of the Savior long before he became a babe in Mary's arms. The brother of Jared's experience isn't strictly a "gospel," then, if we want to define the category narrowly as a narrative of Christ's mortal life. And because the Jaredites' migration to the chosen land preceded the Nephites', the brother of Jared's experience isn't part of the Nephite gospel tradition as it developed in the large plates of Mormon—except when Moroni, in editing the account, explicitly points out connections.

But in other ways, the brother of Jared's encounter with the spirit-bodied Christ shares much in common with Nephite gospels. Reading these seven accounts with you—deeply, one after another—has brought into focus the key features of the Book of Mormon's portrait of Jesus Christ. What has struck me most is their steadfast emphasis on Christ's incarnation, his full human mortality in a body of flesh that is like ours in every respect, particularly in its mortal frailty. Nephi, Benjamin, Abinadi, Alma, Lamoni, Samuel—all testify that Christ came down from heaven and was born of a human mother into a human body. Again and again they affirm that he suffered the pains of body, mind, and soul that afflict his people. His incarnation afforded him the kind of embodied, experiential knowledge that underlies his power to minister to us in our own embodied experience. With his own body, he walked the path of our suffering, our rejoicing, our dying. And Christ's incarnation transforms the meaning of human suffering: because he assumed a body of flesh and blood, when we suffer, we suffer with Christ. When we die, we die with Christ. And when we rise again, we rise in Christ.

I've known each of these passages, of course, and I've loved them individually. But reading them together has surprised me with their powerful cumulative effect. I came to this project with a certain idea in mind, an idea I encountered in an insightful article about the Book of Mormon. Years ago, the theologian Krister Stendahl noticed that the portrait of Christ in 3 Nephi, in which he appears and ministers to the Nephites, resembles the Christ in the gospel of John.[13] Both accounts give us an elevated picture of Christ that emphasizes his divinity and miraculous power at the expense of his human nature. Stendahl's observation is sound, but I had mistakenly generalized the idea to the entire Book of Mormon. I half expected to find in these seven gospels a similarly elevated portrait of Jesus, a superhero Christ who is more divine than human even while he walks the earth. After all, the Nephite people never interacted with Christ during his mortal life and in his mortal body. They conversed and interacted with him only in his pre- and postmortal states.

Not for the first and not for the last time, I was wrong. The Nephite gospels give us a Jesus Christ who is among us, like us, for us, with us, and in us. Yes, we see him working mighty miracles of healing and ministry among his people—but Alma shows us that Christ's healing ministry is less a supernatural marvel than it is the practical knowledge, the "know . . . how," that comes from his own voluntary immersion in our suffering (Alma 7:12). Christ's divine nature never dilutes his full humanity. On the contrary, his divine nature is what allows him to show us what it means to know God in our human condition.

In this way, the brother of Jared's mountaintop encounter with Christ fits beautifully with the six other gospels in the Book of Mormon. In fact, it dramatically underscores their testimony of Christ's humanity. Ether 3 shows us that even in his divine premortal state, before he came down from heaven to be among his people, as the gospels testified he would, Christ was already like us. Rather than existing as an immaterial principle or personality, the premortal Christ existed as a body—a body of spirit, we're told, that surely differed in some material respects from the mortal body he would assume at birth. But spirit bodies seem to share most of what is central to any kind of body. Christ's spirit body appears on Mount Shelem in a form that is bounded and distinct, with particular characteristics that the brother of Jared recognizes as human (Ether 3:15–16). His spirit body is composed of different parts, individual elements that work together but are also capable of working separately, as when his finger touches the stones with divine light (Ether 3:6). Later, Moroni tells us that Christ appeared to the brother of Jared "after the manner and in the likeness of the same body even as he showed himself unto the Nephites" (Ether 3:17). And this may suggest that Christ's spirit body already prefigured the marks of his crucifixion, the open wounds in his hands, feet, and side that the Nephites felt one by one (3 Nephi 11:15).

These properties of bodies—their boundedness and particularity, their complex construction and their openness—are so familiar to us that we hardly recognize them, except when they frustrate our plans or immerse us in pain. Our bodies' flesh-and-spirit materiality is the water we swim in. My body's boundedness is what allows me to know other people as separate from me and thus to experience the joy of love and the pain of grief in my relationships with husband, parents, siblings, and friends. My body's particularity, my female physiology and brain, is what allowed me to bear my four beloved children and also what plunged me into a harrowing postpartum depression after each birth. My body's complex divisibility and openness is what allowed me to nurse three of my children, sharing with them everything from my stem cells to my antibodies, and also to pour my heart out in worry and work to nourish the fourth when I couldn't nurse him.

My body's limitations and capacities, two sides of the same coin, structure the way I move through the world in hundreds of ways, not only familial and reproductive but social and political, personal and communal, ordinary and extraordinary. Jesus Christ's appearance to the brother of Jared affirms the blessedness of my body—the potential of my bodily weakness and capacity to be turned to godly ends—because it shows me that I am "created after [his] own image" from the beginning (Ether 3:15). Christ on Mount Shelem shows me what a human body is, and *why* it is what it is. In turn, Christ in the gospels shows me what a body is for: to minister, to suffer, to dwell with, to learn how, to take upon, to die, and to come forth.

Rosalynde

"Behold, this body, which ye now behold, is the body of my spirit; and man have I created after the body of my spirit; and even as I appear unto thee to be in the spirit will I appear unto my people in the flesh." (Ether 3:16)

Rosalynde,

All of this is well said.

It's been a joy sharing this work with you. I love reading. And I especially love reading with friends.

I'm reminded of the salutation revealed in 1832 for use in the School of the Prophets. The members of the school were instructed to greet each other in the following way: "I salute you in the name of the Lord Jesus Christ, in token or remembrance of the everlasting covenant, in which covenant I receive you to fellowship, in a determination that is fixed, immovable, and unchangeable, to be your friend and brother through the grace of God in the bonds of love, to walk in all the commandments of God blameless, in thanksgiving, forever and ever. Amen" (Doctrine and Covenants 88:133).

I'm glad to greet you in the same way, fixed and immovable in my determination to be your friend and brother in Christ.

With respect to Ether 3, I think you're right to ask if there isn't something different about the brother of Jared's account of the gospel—different enough that we should ask whether it *is* a gospel in the same sense as the others.

Where our other prophets were insulated from the shock of God's full glory through the preparatory mediation of visions, angels, and texts, the brother of Jared isn't. Empowered by some potent combination of deep faith, frank innocence, and compelling humility, the brother of Jared reaches straight through the veil and immediately grasps the live wire of divinity with both bare hands.

What others see in vision, hear from angels, or glean from prophecies, the brother of Jared sees with his own eyes.

Where others bear witness *about* the coming Christ, the brother of Jared *meets* Christ.

And, like you, I'm struck by how embodied and *fleshy* this encounter already seems to be, long before Christ's condescension and incarnation. When the brother of Jared parts the veil, he's greeted by Christ's anticipatory body, by a spirit body modeled on flesh. He's greeted by a body that already shows itself as material, as bounded and particular, as complex and divisible and porous—a body that, despite being spirit, already belongs to our world of resistance and friction and gravity.

"Never have I showed myself unto man whom I have created," the Lord tells the brother of Jared, "for never has man believed in me as thou hast" (Ether 3:15). And then of this body the Lord says: "Behold, this body, which ye now behold, is the body of my spirit; and man have I created after the body of my spirit; and even as I appear unto thee to be in the spirit will I appear unto my people in the flesh" (Ether 3:16).

But what, exactly, did the brother of Jared then see? What happened when he met the premortal Christ?

With you, I favor a strong reading of Moroni's description.

Of their actual meeting, Moroni says just this: "that Jesus showed himself unto this man in the spirit, even after the manner and in the likeness of the same body even as he showed himself unto the Nephites. And he ministered unto him even as he ministered unto the Nephites; and all this, that this man might know that he was God, because of the many great works which the Lord had showed unto him" (Ether 3:17–18).

We could, of course, offer a bare-bones reading of these verses as some scholars and Church leaders have done.[14] We could take them to mean only that the brother of Jared saw the same basic person as the Nephites. In *Christ and the New Covenant,* for instance, Elder Jeffrey R. Holland acknowledges the reality of a range of possible readings for this vision, while also suggesting that "another interpretation of this passage is that the faith of the brother of Jared was so great he saw not only the *spirit* finger and body of the premortal Jesus (which presumably many other prophets had also seen) but also some distinctly more revealing aspect of Christ's body of flesh, blood, and bone."[15]

Especially in light of Elder Holland's suggestion, I'm inclined to think that the specificity of Moroni's description encourages more than a bare-bones reading. Jesus, Moroni emphasizes, showed himself to the brother of Jared "after the *manner* and in the likeness of the *same* body" he showed the Nephites.

Which "same" body did Jesus show the Nephites?

That body is quite specific. Christ showed the Nephites a resurrected body with "the prints of the nails" in his hands and feet and an open wound in his side (3 Nephi 11:14).

And in what "manner" were the Nephites shown this body?

That manner is also quite specific. The Nephites were commanded to "thrust their hands into his side" and "feel the prints of the nails in his hands and in his feet; and this they did do, going forth one by one until they had all gone forth, and did see with their eyes and did feel with their hands, and did know of a surety" (3 Nephi 11:15).

On my reading, Moroni's use of this same description in Ether 3 strongly implies that the brother of Jared saw, in advance, this same crucified-but-resurrected body. And, too, I think this description strongly implies that the brother of Jared's "manner" of witnessing this body involved feeling for himself, just as the Nephites did, those same wounds in Christ's hands, feet, and side.

Here, it seems to me, Christ's body isn't presented to the brother of Jared in the image of an unharmed and invulnerable spirit. Rather, just the opposite: Christ's spirit body already bears the image of his crucified-but-resurrected flesh.

Somehow, even before the world's creation, Christ was already "the Lamb slain from the foundation of the world" (Revelation 13:8). And somehow, even before he was born, Christ had already inscribed his love for us on the palms of his hands: "Can a woman forget her sucking child, that she should not have compassion on the son of her womb? yea, they may forget, yet will I not forget thee. Behold, I have graven thee upon the palms of my hands" (Isaiah 49:15–16).

In this way, Christ's spirit body reveals something fundamental about all bodies. Christ's premortal body shows itself as already related and relational, as already wounded and vulnerable, as already entangled across space and time with its own past and future. His body shows itself as already stretched beyond its own borders, as already more than just itself.

In this way, as you've emphasized, Christ's body is no special case. Christ's body, already in relation to both its own future and our present bodies, is like our own.

And in this way, Christ's body is also like the brother of Jared's.

Like many readers of Ether 3, I love that Moroni's summary never directly reveals the brother of Jared's name. Jared, we know. Jared is named. But his brother, despite his centrality to the story, is just Jared's brother.

The brother of Jared isn't defined by his own name. He isn't defined by his own identity. The brother of Jared is defined by his *relationship* with someone else.

Despite the fact that this is true for everyone, this is a truth that's easy to overlook.

People aren't islands. They aren't closed systems. They aren't self-contained wholes that must then find some way to escape themselves, to break through their shells, enter into relationships, and connect with the world around them. (Though the *illusion* that we're islands—that we're stranded and walled off and alone—is a predictable side effect of being a sinner.)

The truth is just the opposite. Relationships between people *create* people. (Where would I be without my father and mother loving one another?) And people, in turn, grow and change and progress only by way of that same expanding web of relationships.

People are relational all the way down.

If you could unwind me, layer by layer, to reveal the core of who I am, you wouldn't find a little self-contained "Adam" at my center, indivisible and autonomous, pulling the levers. Instead, you'd find my father and mother, my wife and children, my ward members and mission companions, my teachers and students, my friends and enemies—and, especially, my God and his Christ.

Our relationships—together with our loving or fearful responses to those relationships—make us who we are.

My relationships make me who I am: son of Kay, husband of Gwen, brother of Anne, father of Nathan, friend of Rosalynde, disciple of Christ.

As Jesus liked to say, at the last day "ye shall know that I am in my Father, and ye in me, and I in you" (John 14:20).

And these same kinds of relationships make the brother of Jared who he is: not simply himself, but the *brother* of Jared.

Perhaps this is what fits the brother of Jared for his early encounter with Christ, the fact that he is already outside of himself, already more than himself. The fact that the brother of Jared already wears his true relational nature on his sleeve and in his name.

It may also be, though, that we do know something, albeit obliquely, about the brother of Jared's own proper name. Many

Latter-day Saints have heard some version of the following story about Joseph Smith, here reported by George Reynolds:

> While residing in Kirtland Elder Reynolds Cahoon had a son born to him. One day when President Joseph Smith was passing his door, he called the Prophet in and asked him to bless and name the baby. Joseph did so and gave the boy the name of Mahonri Moriancumer. When he had finished the blessing he laid the child on the bed, and turning to Elder Cahoon he said, "The name I have given your son is the name of the brother of Jared; the Lord has just shown [or revealed] it to me." Elder William F. Cahoon, who was standing near, heard the Prophet make this statement to his father; and this was the first time the name of the brother of Jared was known in the Church in this dispensation.[16]

My own thinking about this story was memorably shaped in a Book of Mormon class I had at BYU as an undergrad. When I got home from my mission in Albuquerque, I was hungry to learn everything I could about our scriptures. After sampling a couple of different religion classes, I found what I was looking for: a class with Joseph Fielding McConkie, son of Elder Bruce R. McConkie and grandson of President Joseph Fielding Smith. Brother McConkie had his father's baritone voice, his father's apostolic conviction about Christ and the Restoration, and his father's deep familiarity with our scriptures. I won't pretend that Brother McConkie's classes were for everyone, but they were for me. And after that first class with him, I came back again and again, taking every class he offered.

One day in a Book of Mormon class, Brother McConkie shared his—as always, adamantly expressed—opinion about the idea that the brother of Jared's name was Mahonri Moriancumer. This is only partly true, he said. No one in the Book of Mormon has a first and last name. In the Book of Mormon, people have only one name.

Mahonri, he argued, is the name given by Joseph Smith to the baby. It's not the brother of Jared's name. The brother of Jared's name is just Moriancumer.

And then, as always, he said he'd prove it from the Book of Mormon.

He had us turn to Ether 2:13: "And as they came to the sea they pitched their tents; and they called the name of the place Moriancumer." And then he pointed to the cross-reference at the bottom of the page: "Now it was the custom of the people of Nephi to call their lands, and their cities, and their villages, yea, even all their small villages, after the name of him who first possessed them" (Alma 8:7).

This argument may not be as airtight as Brother McConkie presented it, but I've always remembered it and I've always found it persuasive.

I like the simplicity of just one name: Moriancumer. I like the fact that this name is hidden in plain sight in the Book of Mormon itself. And, especially, I love that when Moroni sneaks this name into his record, he associates it with a *place*, not a person.

This, I'll claim, is not just good poetry but good anthropology. People, ultimately, are more like places than things. People are more like a "there" than an "it."

As German philosopher Martin Heidegger liked to say, people are a kind of "being-there." Each person's body is a site, a ground, a locus, a crossroads. Each person's body is a meeting place where many lives intertwine, where many relationships take root, where new lives are born, where heaven and earth meet.

The brother of Jared's gospel is distinguished by the fact that he *meets* Christ. But the man himself is defined by his relationships and the space he makes for them. The brother of Jared's life isn't about himself, it's about the people he's with. Perhaps, then, it's no surprise that he can give place to God, that he can make so much room for God to show so much of himself.

And, perhaps, this is what it always means to be given a gospel and commissioned to bear the good news of God's arrival.

The gospel according to Mary—or Nephi, Benjamin, Abinadi, Alma, Abish, Samuel, or the brother of Jared—is God's good news as it appears at the unique crossroads of that person's singular life.

To be a disciple of Christ is to lean into this same work of being a "there" for God's arrival. To be a disciple is to devote yourself to the work of making space for God to not only show himself to you but in you and through you.

I hope that, in some small ways, we've been part of that same work in this book. I hope that, especially working together, we've been able to make a little more space for God to show himself than we ever could have working alone.

"Come, Lord Jesus" (Revelation 22:20).

Come!

Adam

— CONCLUSION —

When I, Rosalynde, was a child, every Sunday morning took me to an old meetinghouse at the end of a palm-lined avenue. It had been hand-built by the original ward members in the faux-Tudor style favored by the Saints in Los Angeles at the turn of the last century. Above the pulpit, the builders installed a stained-glass window of Christ. The window harvested a soft southern light all year. My earliest image of Jesus came from those glowing panes, dozens of delicate pieces soldered in the form of a man holding a lantern, knocking at a door.

In this book, we've offered metaphors for our seven gospel witnesses of Christ. We've talked of voices in a chorus, each bringing its unique properties to the common project of preaching "Jesus Christ, and him crucified" (1 Corinthians 2:2). Stained glass joins this small collection of metaphors. Each individual pane, like each of the accounts we've read here, bears a different shape and color and depicts a different portion of the image. Alone, each piece is incomplete; together, they approach a fuller representation of Christ's radiance.

What image of Christ appears when we assemble our seven panes and step back to take in the full view? Each gospel gives us a picture, a promise, and an invitation.

The gospel of Mary, tumbled through the imagery of Nephi's

vision, shows us the Son of God as a babe in arms, embodying the condescension of God as he comes down from heaven and goes forth in solidarity with the human family. Mary's gospel promises that we can experience a union with God that is as sweet and joyfully radiant as the fruit of Lehi's tree. Through the figure of Mary, it invites us to live as the recipients and the givers of God's love.

The gospel of Benjamin shows us the Lord Omnipotent, the Father and Creator of all, who was willing to come down from heaven to inhabit a body as vulnerable as Benjamin's own failing tabernacle. Benjamin's gospel promises that our natural fear and rage in suffering can be redeemed according to the pattern of Christ's own patience before death. This gospel, with its two-stroke heartbeat of divine power and divine meekness, invites us to follow Christ in laying our lives on the altar of sacrifice as a holy offering rather than a bitter cup.

The gospel of Abinadi, with the untamed soul of a poet, shows us "God himself" as the suffering servant, the Son who modeled silence and submission in the face of the awful price of redemption. This Jesus suffered physical infirmity, yes, but more deeply he "suffered" the will of the Father by making peace with what life and death required of him. This gospel promises, paradoxically, that Christ in his meekness defeated death itself, and that all will rise and sing together in the Resurrection. Abinadi's gospel invites us to consecrate our will as Christ did, by suffering, unyieldingly, the submission of our own flesh and spirit to the Father.

The gospel of Alma shows us a Redeemer who left his high station and came in love, not judgment, to be with his people—just as Alma himself did in imitation of Christ. Alma's gospel promises that, by taking on a human body, Christ also took on human suffering, sin, and death so that he would know, in his flesh and in his bones, how to help us. This is the real miracle of Christ's ministry, Alma teaches. Christ invites us to be born again—rising from sin, as from the waters of baptism, into the kingdom of God that is everywhere at hand.

The gospel of Abish shows us a radiant Jesus and how the barest mention of his coming is enough to flood with light the hearts of those who turn to him. It promises that a new King has established a new kingdom, a place where the servant precedes the queen in knowledge of the gospel and the low raise the lofty in reflection of Christ's life and love. This gospel invites us into conversion's dawning awareness that true joy is always shared with others and that true light always reveals our reliance on God.

The gospel of Samuel gives us a split-screen view of the Lord Jesus Christ, juxtaposing the order of creation and the order of redemption in the bright day of his birth and the long night of his death. Its promise of Christ's imminent coming looks like a warning of vengeance when read in the blacklight of sin's shame and avoidance. But Samuel's gospel invites us to look up in faith, not in fear, and to trust the signs of Christ's unfailing love.

The gospel of Jared's brother shows us the spirit body of Jesus Christ and affirms the fundamental goodness of flesh, including the human body that Christ assumes at his mortal birth and the bodies with which we follow him and love one another. The gospel of the brother of Jared promises that Christ brings his sons and daughters back into his presence, where we see, engraved in his glorified flesh, his love for us. This gospel invites us to see ourselves in Christ's image, as a meeting place for the covenant relationships that shape us.

Each of these witnesses seeks an adequate language for the image of Jesus visible in the countenance of the saints themselves as the collective body of Christ. Their testimonies give us the voices of men and angels, mothers and fathers, preachers and converts, kings and servants. Their glad tidings go forth in private and public places, in bedrooms and throne rooms, on towers and walls, in valleys and on mountaintops. The good news comes in the shape of sermons, visions, poems, enacted experience, and even cosmic signs that dance among the stars. Each combination of voice, setting, and form speaks with special urgency to different readers at different times. Each pane of glass contributes in its particular way to the Book of Mormon's radiant picture of Christ.

The stained-glass image of Jesus that stands over the pulpit in my hometown meetinghouse shows him knocking at a door with no handle. It's an allusion to the saying of Christ in the book of Revelation, "Behold, I stand at the door, and knock: if any man hear my voice, and open the door, I will come in to him, and will sup with him, and he with me" (Revelation 3:20). The image is an invitation in itself, an echo of Christ's words. He invites us to do more than simply observe him at a distance. He calls us to open our hearts and minds to commune with him.

For all their diversity, these seven testimonies share that common aim. Unlike ordinary biographies, gospels seek to do more than impart information. Gospels call us to saving faith in Jesus Christ. The author's every rhetorical and historical choice must serve that aim. As the author of the gospel of John puts it, "These are written, that ye might believe that Jesus is the Christ, the Son of God; and that believing ye might have life through his name" (John 20:31). Or as Nephi puts it, "We labor diligently to write, to persuade our children, and also our brethren, to believe in Christ" (2 Nephi 25:23). Or again, as Mormon puts it, "Lay hold upon the gospel of Christ, which shall be set before you, not only in [the Book of Mormon] but also in [the Bible]. . . . For behold, this is written for the intent that ye may believe" (Mormon 7:8–9). These witnesses lay their pearls before the world in order to receive a response of faith, a faith which brings salvation.

Our own writings in this book, these few letters between friends, have a much more modest aim. Of ourselves, we hope only to have pointed you back to the scriptures, to have touched on a few of their treasures, and to have modeled the joyful practice of shared reading. We affirm the apostolic words of Elder Joseph B. Wirthlin, who asked, quoting 1 John 5:3, "Do you love the Lord? Spend time with Him. Meditate on His words. Take His yoke upon you. Seek to understand and obey, because 'this is the love of God, that we keep his commandments.'"[17]

Christ stands at the threshold and knocks. He enters to any and all who hear his voice, who reach for the door. If you open, he will come in to you.

— NOTES —

Book epigraph: Clark G. Gilbert, "Becoming More in Christ: The Parable of the Slope" (general conference address, October 2021).

1. Ezra Taft Benson, "The Book of Mormon—Keystone of Our Religion" (general conference address, October 1986).
2. Neal A. Maxwell, "The Disciple-Scholar," in *On Becoming a Disciple-Scholar*, ed. Henry B. Eyring (Salt Lake City: Bookcraft, 1995), 7.
3. Gordon B. Hinckley, "The Empty Tomb Bore Testimony" (general conference address, April 1988).
4. As used in this book, the phrase "the gospel of Mary" refers only to Mary's own witness of the gospel as presented in our canonized scriptures, especially in 1 Nephi 11. No reference is intended to the text of any noncanonical gospels of Mary that may exist outside our standard works.
5. "Once in Royal David's City," *Hymns*, no. 205.
6. Adam Miller, *Original Grace: An Experiment in Restoration Thinking* (Salt Lake City: Deseret Book, 2022), 25–31.
7. Quotations from poetry by Dylan Thomas ("Do Not Go Gentle into That Good Night") and Edna St. Vincent Millay ("Dirge without Music").
8. See Joseph M. Spencer, "Isaiah 52 in the Book of Mormon: Notes on Isaiah's Reception History," in *The Anatomy of Book of Mormon Theology*, vol. 2 (Salt Lake City, UT: Greg Kofford Books, 2021), 182–91.
9. For a full exploration of the parallels between Alma 19 and John 11, see Nicholas J. Frederick and Joseph M. Spencer, "John 11 in the Book of Mormon," *Journal of the Bible and Its Reception* 5, no. 1 (2018): 81–105.
10. Adam Miller, *An Early Resurrection: Life in Christ Before You Die* (Provo, UT: Neal A. Maxwell Institute; Salt Lake City: Deseret Book, 2018).
11. John W. Welch, "Textual Consistency," in *Reexploring the Book of Mormon*, ed. John W. Welch (Provo, UT: Foundation for Ancient Research and Mormon Studies; Salt Lake City: Deseret Book, 1992), 21–22.
12. Miller, *Original Grace*, 38.
13. Krister Stendahl, "The Sermon on the Mount and Third Nephi," in *Reflections on Mormonism: Judaeo-Christian Parallels*, ed. Truman G. Madsen

(Provo, UT: Religious Studies Center, Brigham Young University, 1978), 139–54.

14. Harold B. Lee wrote that the brother of Jared "saw the kind of body that [Jesus Christ] would have when He came down to the earth." Quoted in Kent P. Jackson, "'Never Have I Showed Myself unto Man': A Suggestion for Understanding Ether 3:15a," *Brigham Young University Studies* 30, no. 3 (1990): 75, note 7. Citing this quotation, two scholars suggest that President Lee meant that the brother of Jared "saw a vision of Christ as his body would be during his mortal ministry." See Joseph Fielding McConkie, Robert L. Millet, and Brent L. Top, *Doctrinal Commentary on the Book of Mormon*, vol. 4 (Salt Lake City: Bookcraft, 1992), 277.
15. Jeffrey R. Holland, *Christ and the New Covenant: The Messianic Message of the Book of Mormon* (Salt Lake City: Deseret Book, 1997), 22.
16. George Reynolds, "The Jaredites," *The Juvenile Instructor* 27, no. 9 (May 1, 1892): 282, note [1].
17. Joseph B. Wirthlin, "The Great Commandment" (general conference address, October 2007).

— INDEX —

INDEX

INDEX

INDEX

— ABOUT THE AUTHORS —

Photo by Jennifer Griffith

ADAM S. MILLER is a professor of philosophy at Collin College in McKinney, Texas. He earned a BA in comparative literature from Brigham Young University and an MA and PhD in philosophy from Villanova University. He is the author of more than ten books, including three copublications with Deseret Book and the Maxwell Institute, *Letters to a Young Mormon*, *An Early Resurrection*, and *Original Grace*. He also directs the Latter-day Saint Theology Seminar.

Photo by Justin Goodson

ROSALYNDE F. WELCH is a senior research fellow and associate director at the Neal A. Maxwell Institute for Religious Scholarship at Brigham Young University. She holds a BA in English from BYU and a PhD in early modern English literature from the University of California San Diego. Welch is an independent scholar working in Latter-day Saint literature, culture, and theology. She is the author of numerous articles on Latter-day Saint theology and scripture. She is the author of *Ether: A Brief Theological Introduction* and the editor of the forthcoming *Are We Not All Beggars? Reading Mosiah 4*.